The Vision of the Patriarchs

Messages to Us from Revealed Insights of the Jewish Pioneers

Mike Brown

Written by: Mike Brown

Published by OneHope Publishing
Facebook: Books by Mike Brown, OneHope Publishing
Printed by Kindle Direct Publishing, an Amazon.com Company
Available from Amazon.com, and other retail outlets

Appreciation is expressed to Cheryl Brown, Sherrie Davidson, and Steve Perryman for their significant support in proofreading and editing.

Cover Design: Mike Brown

Scripture quotations marked (ESV) are taken from the ESV® Bible (The Holy Bible, English Standard Version®), copyright © 2001 by Crossway, a publishing ministry of Good News Publishers. Used by permission. All rights reserved."

Scripture quotations marked (NIV2011) are taken from the Holy Bible, New International Version®, NIV®. Copyright © 1973, 1978, 1984, 2011 by Biblica, Inc.™ Used by permission of Zondervan. All rights reserved worldwide.

Scripture quotations marked (NKJV) are taken from the New King James Version®. Copyright © 1982 by Thomas Nelson. Used by permission. All rights reserved.

Copyright © 2016 - Mike Brown

All rights reserved under International Copyright Law. Permission is granted to copy exerts from this book for non-profit usage, not exceeding 600 words, so long as such copy does not violate scripture copyrights.

ISBN-978-0-9976300-2-2

Cover Art

I am most humbled and very appreciative to Rachel Wimpey for permission to incorporate her wonderful painting on the front cover. I first saw it in her studio while working on the first draft of this book. I was immediately captured by its visual parallel with the message of my book. Rachel is an international artist and gallery owner based in Tulsa, Oklahoma. Her portraits, murals, and biblical subjects can be seen across the globe in many private and university collections. Her biblical works, such as *Man of God* on the cover, often explore the theme of connecting the past to the present, as noted in her style and subject matter. Rachel seeks to build a visual context for people to connect the history of the Bible to their everyday lives and better understand their heritage.

Scripture Formatting
In order to make this study as readable as possible, scripture text is included in the book text. Scriptural quotations are indented and italicized to clearly identify them, like this:

John 8:56 (NIV2011)
⁵⁶ Your father Abraham rejoiced at the thought of seeing my day; he saw it and was glad."

Scripture quoted as part of the commentary text is italicized without quotation marks, like this: 'In the Genesis 15 passage we read *Abram believed the LORD . . .*'

Other Books by this Author:

❖   Celebrating God's Purpose for the Ages
Drawing Nearer to the God of Origin and Eternal Destiny Through Bible Prophecy (2016 2nd edition, paperback 440 pages, available on Amazon, ISBN-978-0-9976300-0-8)

❖   The Mysterious Magi of Christmas
Renewing the Christmas Mystique by Distinguishing the Biblical from the Traditional (2016 paperback 40 pages, available on Amazon, ISBN-978-0-9976300-1-5)

❖   Something to Boast About
A Biblical Perspective on pride and humility and on the priority of knowing God (2018 55 pages, available on Amazon, ISBN-978-0-9976300-3-9)

CONTENTS

Chapter	Page No.
Preface	
1 The Call of Abraham	1
2 Priest of the Most High	17
3 The Unthinkable Test	36
4 The Heart of the Sacrifice	48
5 The Dream	54
6 The Wrestler	60
7 The Patriarchs Still Speak	75

PREFACE

Have you ever wondered, 'What is the purpose, the message, of the Old Testament? Is the Old Testament a critical part of God's plan, or perhaps just a failed plan A? Is there a unifying theme that connects the Old and New Testaments?'

There is indeed a singular theme that wraps both testaments into a comprehensive revelation of God's purpose. The Bible is about one overarching theme: redemption. The Old Testament explains the need and anticipates that redemption. God's redemptive agenda is not a nebulous philosophy. Scripture chronicles and explains God's patient and purposeful process, built around His revelation of Himself and His plan. It is set in the context of verifiable human history. From the beginning, God has orchestrated his plan. The patriarchs of Israel were called out by God to be the founding pilgrims who paved the way for everything that followed in God's redemptive agenda. The Old Testament chronicles the birth of a messianic nation which would birth God's Messiah.

Romans 9:4-5 (NIV2011)
[4] the people of Israel. Theirs is the adoption to sonship; theirs the divine glory, the covenants, the receiving of the law, the temple worship and the promises. [5] Theirs are the patriarchs, and from them is traced the human ancestry of the Messiah, who is God over all, forever praised! Amen.

The life, death and resurrection of Jesus as presented in the four gospels is the focal point in redemptive strategy. Although the Christian faith is focused on Jesus, it is rooted in the formative narratives of the Old Testament. Understanding God's intervention in the lives of the patriarchs significantly aids our comprehension of how His New Testament salvation fits within His grand plan. This book looks at the lives of Abraham, Isaac and Jacob to better understand the extent of revelation God gave to them. We will combine the Genesis narratives with other Old and New Testament references to those same events to broaden our insight into the vision given to these patriarchs and to us.

This is not a comprehensive commentary on the lives of the patriarchs. Rather, it selects certain specific events from the patriarch's lives that speak to us today. God has revealed Himself in ages past in many ways: through divine encounters, through prophecy, through symbolic Hebrew worship practices ordained by God, and through emblematic historic events in the life of the Hebrew nation. This book looks at some of those historic events to discover what God was and is revealing through them about His Messiah.

My hoped-for result will be our greater appreciation of God's grand purpose in redemption, allowing us to comprehend its enormity, its wonder, its glorious beauty and its inexpressible benefit to us. I pray that this study would not be simply an informative study, but also a devotional journey. That our worship would be elevated and our love for God be inflated, so that we might better be prepared for the calling to which he has called us. Also, that it would be a practical one as we apply redemption's purpose to our lives, helping shape our vista-view of life--this life and life eternal.

> *Romans 15:4 (ESV)*
> *[4] For whatever was written in former days was written for our instruction, that through endurance and through the encouragement of the Scriptures we might have hope.*

> *1 Corinthians 10:11 (ESV)*
> *[11] Now these things happened to them as an example, but they were written down for our instruction, on whom the end of the ages has come.*

Chapter 1
The Call of Abraham

Matthew 13:16-17 (NKJV)
¹⁶ *"But blessed are your eyes for they see, and your ears for they hear;* ¹⁷ *for assuredly, I say to you that many prophets and righteous men desired to see what you see, and did not see it, and to hear what you hear, and did not hear it.*

To his disciples, Jesus gave this wonderful and insightful statement. He was telling them how privileged they were. Why were they so privileged? It was because they were seeing firsthand the fulfillment of what the prophets had only seen in shadows. The Old Testament had been pointing its readers forward to a future time, and now that time had come. It was at this very time in human history that God personally entered this creation. In Jesus, God was invading the spiritual dominions in this dark world. The source of salvation was dwelling among men.

The *righteous men* referred to in this scripture were the faithful men and women of the Old Testament. The statement harkens back to and beyond the prophets, sweeping all the way back to the patriarchs of Israel. The world of the patriarch's day was sinful and idolatrous. God had a plan for redemption and rescue. To bring it about, He called a new nation into existence by calling to one man: Abram. From this one man, God would create this very special and unique nation. From this nation would come a deliverer, the Messiah. That is why the people of Jesus' day were so privileged. They were in the very presence of Messiah!

A Messianic Lineage
The family lineage from Adam to Abraham to King David to Jesus is a major theme in Old Testament theology. We Gentiles may find reading genealogies less than invigorating, but every Jew of Jesus' day knew the importance of the doctrine of the messianic lineage. This lineage was initiated by God and first revealed in His pronouncement of the curse upon the serpent (Satan) back in Genesis.

> *Genesis 3:15 (NKJV)*
> *¹⁵ And I will put enmity Between you and the woman, And between your seed and her Seed; He shall bruise your head, And you shall bruise His heel."*

The term *her seed* refers to Jesus. Jesus was an offspring of Eve and Adam. Abram was in this lineage. This is made clear in Paul's New Testament letter to the Galatians.

> *Galatians 3:16 (NIV2011)*
> *¹⁶ The promises were spoken to Abraham and to his seed. Scripture does not say "and to seeds," meaning many people, but "and to your seed," meaning one person, who is Christ.*

Thus, a messianic lineage is proclaimed from the very beginning. There are many people in that lineage, and we can read about them name-by-name in the genealogies of Matthew 1 (Joseph's lineage) and Luke 3 (Mary's lineage). (Even though Joseph was not Jesus' genetic father from a covenant viewpoint, he was his legal father in his culture. Thus both lineages are significant.) There are some very intriguing aspects to the lineages, but we won't focus on those details. Note, however, that there are key people in those lineages. After Adam, the first key figure is Abram, later renamed Abraham.

Now we may be inclined to see Abraham as an obedient responder who unwittingly was playing out a role in God's plan. We might assume he only knew what is told us in the Genesis narrative and that he was blind to the long-range implications of what he was being called to. This might be inferred from the message of our opening scripture. However, Jesus also made the following statement to the religious leaders of his day.

> *John 8:56 (NIV2011)*
> *⁵⁶ Your father Abraham rejoiced at the thought of seeing my day; he saw it and was glad."*

This raises the question, 'How much did Abraham and his offspring know and understand? How extensive was the vision given to Abraham? Perhaps we cannot know precisely, but we can learn something of it from the many references made to it throughout scripture.

Abraham's Faith
Let us begin by reading the Genesis narrative of the calling of Abram by God.

> *Genesis 12:1-4 (NKJV)*
> *[1] Now the LORD had said to Abram: "Get out of your country, From your family And from your father's house, To a land that I will show you. [2] I will make you a great nation; I will bless you And make your name great; And you shall be a blessing. [3] I will bless those who bless you, And I will curse him who curses you; And in you all the families of the earth shall be blessed." [4] So Abram departed as the LORD had spoken to him, and Lot went with him. And Abram was seventy-five years old when he departed from Haran.*

Later, God came to Abram and renewed the promise he had made with him. More than renewing it, He confirmed it in a most unusual way, known today as the Abrahamic Covenant.

> *Genesis 15:6-18 (ESV)*
> *[6] And he believed the LORD, and he counted it to him as righteousness. [7] And he said to him, "I am the LORD who brought you out from Ur of the Chaldeans to give you this land to possess." [8] But he said, "O Lord GOD, how am I to know that I shall possess it?" [9] He said to him, "Bring me a heifer three years old, a female goat three years old, a ram three years old, a turtledove, and a young pigeon." [10] And he brought him all these, cut them in half, and laid each half over against the other. But he did not cut the birds in half. [11] And when birds of prey came down on the carcasses, Abram drove them away. [12] As the sun was going down, a deep sleep fell on Abram. And behold, dreadful and great darkness fell upon him. [13] Then the LORD said to Abram, "Know for certain that your offspring will be sojourners in a land that is not theirs and will be servants there, and they will be afflicted for four hundred years. [14] But I will bring judgment on the nation that they serve, and afterward they shall come out with great possessions. [15] As for you, you shall go to your fathers in peace; you shall be buried in a good old age. [16] And they shall come back here in the fourth generation, for the iniquity of the Amorites is not yet complete." [17] When the sun had gone down and it was dark, behold, a smoking fire pot and a*

> *flaming torch passed between these pieces.* [18] *On that day the LORD made a covenant with Abram, saying, "To your offspring I give this land, from the river of Egypt to the great river, the river Euphrates,*

The procedure of cutting animals in half and lining up the halves separated from each other was a way to legalize a covenant in that culture. There were no courts, no judges, no established legality to bring enforcement. So, to add a gravity of obligation to a simple promise, this strange practice was observed. In the process, the two parties would both walk between the carcass halves. This sealed their mutual intents and responsibilities already agreed upon. The dead animals symbolized that they were putting their own lives up as surety for fulfillment of the covenant. They were each saying, in effect, "If I fail to fulfill my obligations of this covenant, may it be to me as to these animals."

In this vision, there passed between the carcass halves a smoking firepot and a blazing torch. It seems as if these are two implements together symbolize one entity, God Himself. Only God passed between the carcasses, not Abraham. This covenant, known as the Abrahamic Covenant, was an unconditional covenant. It was not ratified by Abraham, nor dependent on any action from him.

God's Prophetic Confirmation
The Abrahamic covenant had terms to it. The terms were that God would give Abraham all the things He had promised--posterity, land, long life, a blessing to all nations. Abraham's responsibility was that he (and his descendants) would walk in obedience before God. God alone ratified this promise. He did so on the basis of Abraham's faith. God alone passed between the carcass halves. God alone ratified the covenant. Abraham did not participate in ratifying it.

Think about the implications of that fact. In this transaction it appears that God was saying, 'If either of us violate the terms of this covenant, I alone will pay with my life.'

Of course God never violated the covenant, but Abraham did. Everyone who claims to be a genetic or spiritual child of Abraham has also violated it. In light of that, how would God fulfill His end of the covenant? About 1900 years later, God made good on His promise when Jesus died on the cross. The cross of Christ was the payment for the sins of the world, including all the children of

Abraham. It was the fulfillment of the Abrahamic Covenant. This was God's intentional purpose in this covenant. We should not see the cross as drawing significance from this covenant. On the contrary, the covenant draws its significance from the cross. This covenant points forward in symbolism to the real transaction, the cross of Jesus.

Thus, the Abrahamic Covenant set the stage to show the great need and to foreshadow God's grand plan for salvation through Christ's atoning work on the cross.

Heirs Through Faith
Our requirement for being a spiritual heir of Abraham is faith. This covenant with Abraham is referred to in the New Testament repeatedly to demonstrate this single requirement.

Romans 4:3-5 (NIV2011)
[3] What does Scripture say? "Abraham believed God, and it was credited to him as righteousness." [4] Now to the one who works, wages are not credited as a gift but as an obligation. [5] However, to the one who does not work but trusts God who justifies the ungodly, their faith is credited as righteousness.

Hebrews 6:13-18 (ESV)
[13] For when God made a promise to Abraham, since he had no one greater by whom to swear, he swore by himself, [14] saying, "Surely I will bless you and multiply you." [15] And thus Abraham, having patiently waited, obtained the promise. [16] For people swear by something greater than themselves, and in all their disputes an oath is final for confirmation. [17] So when God desired to show more convincingly to the heirs of the promise the unchangeable character of his purpose, he guaranteed it with an oath, [18] so that by two unchangeable things, in which it is impossible for God to lie, we who have fled for refuge might have strong encouragement to hold fast to the hope set before us.

What were the two unchangeable things that are strong encouragement for us? The first was God's promise, which should be enough. The second was God's ratified oath, his guarantee. It is amazing that God would condescend to meet

Abraham's need and overcome his doubts, and that He does the same with ours.

We observe something else in this. In the Genesis 15 passage we read *⁶Abram believed the LORD . . . ⁸But Abram said, "Sovereign LORD, how can I know that I will gain possession of it?"* Here we have a picture of Abraham, the father of the faithful, having less-than-perfect faith. This is rather shocking! Up until now, Abraham has been portrayed as unwavering in his faith, setting the standard for faith. Now he seems almost—well, like us. We are made to realize that his faith, a faith that God accepted, was not perfect faith. We are reminded of the man in the time of Christ whose demon-possessed son Jesus was about to heal.

Mark 9:24 (NIV2011)
²⁴ Immediately the boy's father exclaimed, "I do believe; help me overcome my unbelief!"

Perhaps if we are honest, we identify with that father, and with Abraham. We know our faith is not perfect and that may cause suppressed concern as to whether we are faithful enough to make the cut. Or maybe it is not suppressed. Maybe you have had nagging fears about this. This is comforting to read. God can take faith as small as a mustard seed, and grow it into a full-blown mustard plant large enough for birds to roost in. Come before Almighty God humbly seeking His mercy, and He will enable your faith.

The Patriarchal Heritage

Through the call of Abram the most unique and peculiar nation on earth was initiated with a single family. God claimed this nation to be His special possession. This claim was not based on the righteousness of the people. It was based on God's sovereign selection of them as His chosen people. God blessed Abram and Sarah with a son in their old age. Isaac was the son of the covenant. Isaac had a covenant son of his own in Jacob. This same promise was renewed by God to Isaac (Genesis 26:1-5) and to Jacob (Genesis 28:10-15). Each one was personally given the call. From that time forward, God often distinguished Himself as the God of Abraham, Isaac and Jacob, as in these passages.

Exodus 3:6 (NIV2011)
⁶ Then he said, "I am the God of your father, the God of

Abraham, the God of Isaac and the God of Jacob." At this, Moses hid his face, because he was afraid to look at God.

Exodus 3:14-15 (NIV2011)
[14] God said to Moses, "I AM WHO I AM. This is what you are to say to the Israelites: 'I AM has sent me to you.' " [15] God also said to Moses, "Say to the Israelites, 'The LORD, the God of your fathers—the God of Abraham, the God of Isaac and the God of Jacob—has sent me to you.' "This is my name forever, the name you shall call me from generation to generation.

Matthew 22:31-32 (NIV2011)
[31] But about the resurrection of the dead—have you not read what God said to you, [32] 'I am the God of Abraham, the God of Isaac, and the God of Jacob'? He is not the God of the dead but of the living."

Back to our narrative, God later appeared again to Abram. He repeated His covenant promise with even more detail.

Genesis 17:1-8 (ESV)
[1] When Abram was ninety-nine years old the LORD appeared to Abram and said to him, "I am God Almighty; walk before me, and be blameless, [2] that I may make my covenant between me and you, and may multiply you greatly." [3] Then Abram fell on his face. And God said to him, [4] "Behold, my covenant is with you, and you shall be the father of a multitude of nations. [5] No longer shall your name be called Abram, but your name shall be Abraham, for I have made you the father of a multitude of nations. [6] I will make you exceedingly fruitful, and I will make you into nations, and kings shall come from you. [7] And I will establish my covenant between me and you and your offspring after you throughout their generations for an everlasting covenant, to be God to you and to your offspring after you. [8] And I will give to you and to your offspring after you the land of your sojournings, all the land of Canaan, for an everlasting possession, and I will be their God."

Abraham Remained a Pilgrim
The covenant made by God with Abraham included a posterity of heirs and the inheritance of the land in which they were dwelling. The same terms were promised to Isaac and to Jacob. However,

as we read on through Genesis, the patriarchal families remained a nomadic clan. Wherever they moved, they were aliens. Although they were sometimes on compatible terms with surrounding neighbors, they did not realize ownership of the land.

Eventually the number of this clan began to grow, and a famine brought them into Egypt. For 430 years they remained in Egypt, where they were later enslaved by a new Egyptian dynasty. During their time in Egypt, their numbers increased from a small clan to a number too numerous to count. When they came out of Egypt during the exodus, their population is estimated at around two million. The New Testament writer of Hebrews stated:

> *Hebrews 11:8-9,12-13 (NKJV)*
> *[8] By faith Abraham obeyed when he was called to go out to the place which he would receive as an inheritance. And he went out, not knowing where he was going. [9] By faith he dwelt in the land of promise as in a foreign country, dwelling in tents with Isaac and Jacob, the heirs with him of the same promise; . . . [12] Therefore from one man, and him as good as dead, were born as many as the stars of the sky in multitude--innumerable as the sand which is by the seashore. [13] These all died in faith, not having received the promises, but having seen them afar off were assured of them, embraced them and confessed that they were strangers and pilgrims on the earth.*

> *Isaiah 51:1-2 (NIV2011)*
> *[1] "Listen to me, you who pursue righteousness and who seek the LORD: Look to the rock from which you were cut and to the quarry from which you were hewn; [2] look to Abraham, your father, and to Sarah, who gave you birth. When I called him he was only one man, and I blessed him and made him many.*

The Messianic Objective

As we have noted, the call to Abraham was more than a promise of heirs and lands. It was a call toward eternity. It was not just about eternity for that small called-out group. We now see that this was step-one in a grand plan to bring redemption to the entire world. Also, we have mentioned the messianic lineage, the purpose of which was to spawn the Messiah. The entire Old Testament points forward to the coming of Messiah. That is the underlying theme of the Old Testament. So the blessing of

Abraham was the front-end of a redemptive plan that was fulfilled in the gospels of the New Testament. Jesus is the fulfillment of the whole purpose for the call and progression of the nation of Israel. Apart from him, Israel is just another upstart nation scratching for survival.

Abraham Given Divine Vision

Did God fail to keep His promise to Abraham? Again, the Hebrew writer tells us something very important and central to what we are saying. Speaking of Abraham, he says:

> *Hebrews 11:10-11,13-16 (NIV2011)*
> *[10] For he was looking forward to the city with foundations, whose architect and builder is God. [11] And by faith even Sarah, who was past childbearing age, was enabled to bear children because she considered him faithful who had made the promise . . . [13] All these people were still living by faith when they died. They did not receive the things promised; they only saw them and welcomed them from a distance, admitting that they were foreigners and strangers on earth. [14] People who say such things show that they are looking for a country of their own. [15] If they had been thinking of the country they had left, they would have had opportunity to return. [16] Instead, they were longing for a better country—a heavenly one. Therefore God is not ashamed to be called their God, for he has prepared a city for them.*

The book of Hebrews describes Abraham's understanding as a much more comprehensive scope than just descendants and land, as grand as those were. It describes a promise more enduring than just a long and fulfilling mortal life. It tells us that Abraham understood the promises from an eternal and panoramic perspective. Abraham was looking for an eternal city from God.

Our Eternal Perspective

Abraham saw the fulfillment of God's promises *from a distance*. He lived his earthly life in hope of something never experienced. Because of that hope, and his belief in God's promises, God justified him in his faith. We have much more of God's plan historically revealed to us. Yet in everyday life, we must rely on hope for that which is seen dimly. God may bring glimpses of fulfillment to us to encourage us, but largely we, like Abraham, are called to trust Him. We are called to live a life of hope. We who believe and trust in God's promises are related spiritually to Abraham.

> *Romans 4:16-17 (NIV2011)*
> *¹⁶ Therefore, the promise comes by faith, so that it may be by grace and may be guaranteed to all Abraham's offspring—not only to those who are of the law but also to those who have the faith of Abraham. He is the father of us all. ¹⁷ As it is written: "I have made you a father of many nations." He is our father in the sight of God, in whom he believed—the God who gives life to the dead and calls into being things that were not.*

> *Galatians 3:7-9 (NIV2011)*
> *⁷ Understand, then, that those who have faith are children of Abraham. ⁸ Scripture foresaw that God would justify the Gentiles by faith, and announced the gospel in advance to Abraham: "All nations will be blessed through you. ⁹ So those who rely on faith are blessed along with Abraham, the man of faith.*

> *Galatians 3:29 (NIV2011)*
> *²⁹ If you belong to Christ, then you are Abraham's seed, and heirs according to the promise.*

Even though we are Abraham's spiritual offspring, and he is our spiritual father, yet his ultimate redemption will not take place until ours does. Abraham, Isaac and Jacob and all the other faithful people of the Old Testament will not be fully glorified except with us. Ours is a much greater redemption, not limited to genetic heritage and inherited land. Therefore, God delayed final fulfillment of their promises until they could participate in that greater redemption that we hope for.

> *Hebrews 11:39-40 (NIV2011)*
> *³⁹ These were all commended for their faith, yet none of them received what had been promised, ⁴⁰ since God had planned something better for us so that only together with us would they be made perfect.*

> *Romans 11:28-32 (NKJV)*
> *²⁸ Concerning the gospel they are enemies for your sake, but concerning the election they are beloved for the sake of the fathers. ²⁹ For the gifts and the calling of God are*

irrevocable. ³⁰ For as you were once disobedient to God, yet have now obtained mercy through their disobedience, ³¹ even so these also have now been disobedient, that through the mercy shown you they also may obtain mercy. ³² For God has committed them all to disobedience, that He might have mercy on all.

Messianic Opposition

We can hardly speak about the messianic lineage without recognizing the existence of a significant opposition to this plan of God. This world has been the domain of Satan since his expulsion from heaven. He is called in scripture *the prince of this world* and *the ruler of the kingdom of the air*. Throughout the Old Testament, Satan's main agenda has been to destroy the messianic lineage, and to halt the redemptive objective. He has come very close several times. However, God always made a way of rescue for that lineage, working through providential means to ultimately bring about salvation in Jesus, His Messiah. The evil spiritual agenda to destroy that lineage is portrayed symbolically in the book of Revelation.

Revelation 12:1-5 (NKJV)
¹ Now a great sign appeared in heaven: a woman clothed with the sun, with the moon under her feet, and on her head a garland of twelve stars. ² Then being with child, she cried out in labor and in pain to give birth. ³ And another sign appeared in heaven: behold, a great, fiery red dragon having seven heads and ten horns, and seven diadems on his heads. ⁴ His tail drew a third of the stars of heaven and threw them to the earth. And the dragon stood before the woman who was ready to give birth, to devour her Child as soon as it was born. ⁵ She bore a male Child who was to rule all nations with a rod of iron. And her Child was caught up to God and His throne.

In this vision given to John, the dragon represents Satan and the woman is the nation of Israel. This identity is revealed by the woman clothed with the sun and the moon, and a crown of twelve stars. This represents Jacob, Joseph's mother Rachel, and Jacob's twelve sons. This symbolism would be very cryptic if not for a prophetic dream given to Joseph, Jacob's eleventh son.

> *Genesis 37:9-11 (NIV2011)*
> *⁹ Then he had another dream, and he told it to his brothers. "Listen," he said, "I had another dream, and this time the sun and moon and eleven stars were bowing down to me." ¹⁰ When he told his father as well as his brothers, his father rebuked him and said, "What is this dream you had? Will your mother and I and your brothers actually come and bow down to the ground before you?" ¹¹ His brothers were jealous of him, but his father kept the matter in mind.*

Historically, the prophetic dream was fulfilled in the life of Joseph, but its symbolism is much farther reaching. It identifies for us the woman in the Revelation vision. It is the messianic nation Israel. It was Jacob (later renamed 'Israel') who brought expansion to the patriarchal clan, with his twelve sons who formed the twelve tribes of Israel.

In the Revelation vision, the male child is Jesus. The imagery is the lineage of Israel (formerly Jacob) birthing the Messiah and the devil's attempts to destroy him. The child being *snatched up to God* is a reference to Jesus' resurrection from the dead and subsequent ascension into heaven.

God has permitted the devil to mount opposition to His redemptive purpose, against His messianic lineage. He will not allow that purpose to be defeated. Today the message of God's love and salvation is being taught and heard around the world. Our hope is built on His promise of ultimate victory for all who believe that good news. With Abraham, we look forward to entering that holy heavenly city.

The Heavenly Jerusalem
How much of that heavenly city did Abraham envision and understand? He knew something of it as we have already seen. He may have even understood something about Messiah, since Jesus said:

> *John 8:56 (NIV2011)*
> *⁵⁶ Your father Abraham rejoiced at the thought of seeing my day; he saw it and was glad."*

Like Abraham, we too are waiting for that heavenly city. We too are pilgrims in a foreign world. We too live by faith, in hope.

Philippians 3:20 (NIV2011)
[20] But our citizenship is in heaven. And we eagerly await a Savior from there, the Lord Jesus Christ,

Hebrews 13:14 (NIV2011)
[14] For here we do not have an enduring city, but we are looking for the city that is to come.

Romans 8:22-24 (NIV2011)
[22] We know that the whole creation has been groaning as in the pains of childbirth right up to the present time. [23] Not only so, but we ourselves, who have the firstfruits of the Spirit, groan inwardly as we wait eagerly for our adoption to sonship, the redemption of our bodies. [24] For in this hope we were saved . . .

Thus, we are called to live as foreigners and aliens in this present world. We are called to live in joyful hope, not hoping for a better world in this life, but looking for our heavenly reward. Scripture gives us a jubilant and expectant sneak preview of entering this city. It is a heavenly city. An eternal city.

Hebrews 12:22-24 (NIV2011)
[22] But you have come to Mount Zion, to the city of the living God, the heavenly Jerusalem. You have come to thousands upon thousands of angels in joyful assembly, [23] to the church of the firstborn, whose names are written in heaven. You have come to God, the Judge of all, to the spirits of the righteous made perfect, [24] to Jesus the mediator of a new covenant, and to the sprinkled blood that speaks a better word than the blood of Abel.

As this passage anticipates the heavenly city, it lists all who will be present at that moment, those who will enjoy heaven for eternity. The phrase *the spirits of the righteous made perfect* is a reference to the Old Testament faithful, including the patriarchs. They are made perfect by their resurrection and glorification, which will occur when Jesus calls his own to him. This most majestic scene of heaven includes God, Jesus, angels, the church, and the righteous by faith under the old covenant. It brings us face-to-face with the life-giving blood of the new covenant, in contrast to the blood of Abel which, according to the old covenant, spoke condemnation against his murderer. The blood of Jesus speaks a message of forgiveness and mercy based on a new covenant.

In Revelation we are shown a more detailed vision of this eternal city, given in John's vision.

> *Revelation 21:1-4,9-14,22-24 (NKJV)*
> *[1] Now I saw a new heaven and a new earth, for the first heaven and the first earth had passed away. Also there was no more sea. [2] Then I, John, saw the holy city, New Jerusalem, coming down out of heaven from God, prepared as a bride adorned for her husband. [3] And I heard a loud voice from heaven saying, "Behold, the tabernacle of God is with men, and He will dwell with them, and they shall be His people. God Himself will be with them and be their God. [4] And God will wipe away every tear from their eyes; there shall be no more death, nor sorrow, nor crying. There shall be no more pain, for the former things have passed away." . . . [9] Then one of the seven angels who had the seven bowls filled with the seven last plagues came to me and talked with me, saying, "Come, I will show you the bride, the Lamb's wife." [10] And he carried me away in the Spirit to a great and high mountain, and showed me the great city, the holy Jerusalem, descending out of heaven from God, [11] having the glory of God. Her light was like a most precious stone, like a jasper stone, clear as crystal. [12] Also she had a great and high wall with twelve gates, and twelve angels at the gates, and names written on them, which are the names of the twelve tribes of the children of Israel: [13] three gates on the east, three gates on the north, three gates on the south, and three gates on the west. [14] Now the wall of the city had twelve foundations, and on them were the names of the twelve apostles of the Lamb. . . . [22] But I saw no temple in it, for the Lord God Almighty and the Lamb are its temple. [23] The city had no need of the sun or of the moon to shine in it, for the glory of God illuminated it. The Lamb is its light. [24] And the nations of those who are saved shall walk in its light, and the kings of the earth bring their glory and honor into it.*

Note the foundational symbols of the city are the Old Testament twelve tribes (offspring of the patriarch Jacob), and the twelve New Testament apostles of Christ. The grand redemptive program of God, illuminated in the entire Bible, has been moving in this direction under His hand and in accordance with His purpose.

The crowning source for joy in this scene is that the dwelling of God and of Jesus will be with men. He will wipe away every tear. He will be the light of the city. No longer will we wonder if God really takes note of us. We will be in his presence for all eternity. We will have all eternity to explore his glory, yet never finding its limits.

Our Take-Aways
How much of this imagery was perceived by Abraham remains unclear, but it seems God revealed far more to him than we typically think. He set the standard when it comes to faith. Now, with our more complete view of the big picture from scripture, may we be as faithful with that knowledge as Abraham, Isaac and Jacob were with theirs.

The underlying message for us in this first chapter is the call to live a life of hope. Our circumstances may not encourage hope. Our acquaintances and family may not support a life of hope. Our call is from God Himself, through scripture. We must seek no other source. Paul spoke of this to the Colossians.

> *Colossians 3:1-4 (NKJV)*
> *¹ If then you were raised with Christ, seek those things which are above, where Christ is, sitting at the right hand of God. ² Set your mind on things above, not on things on the earth. ³ For you died, and your life is hidden with Christ in God. ⁴ When Christ who is our life appears, then you also will appear with Him in glory.*

This perspective of eternal priority is spoken of often in the New Testament.

> *1 Peter 2:11 (NIV2011)*
> *¹¹ Dear friends, I urge you, as foreigners and exiles, to abstain from sinful desires, which wage war against your soul.*

> *James 4:4 (NIV2011)*
> *⁴ You adulterous people, don't you know that friendship with the world means enmity against God? Therefore,*

anyone who chooses to be a friend of the world becomes an enemy of God.

1 Peter 1:17-20 (NKJV)
[17] And if you call on the Father, who without partiality judges according to each one's work, conduct yourselves throughout the time of your stay here in fear; [18] knowing that you were not redeemed with corruptible things, like silver or gold, from your aimless conduct received by tradition from your fathers, [19] but with the precious blood of Christ, as of a lamb without blemish and without spot. [20] He indeed was foreordained before the foundation of the world, but was manifest in these last times for you

While we are called to be visitors and foreigners in this world, we are not left without a homeland. At one time we were citizens of this world, and strangers to God. Now, as believers, we have changed our birthright. We have changed our citizenship. Let us not drive our tent pegs too deep. May we learn to live a life of hope.

Ephesians 2:19-20 (NIV2011)
[19] Consequently, you are no longer foreigners and strangers [from God], but fellow citizens with God's people and also members of his household, [20] built on the foundation of the apostles and prophets, with Christ Jesus himself as the chief cornerstone.

Chapter 2
The Priest of God Most High

In the fourteenth chapter of Genesis we read of a battle of two alliances of kings that took place in the area around the Dead Sea. These are kings of small city-states. One of the alliances captured the other, and took the people and possessions. Among those captured was Abram's nephew Lot, along with all his family. Soon, word of this reached Abram, who quickly gathered his small army of 318 trained fighting men, and pursued them. Overtaking them, he defeated them and rescued Lot and all the captured people and possessions. As they were returning home, Abram was met by Melchizedek, one of the most intriguing characters in scripture.

> Genesis 14:17-24 (ESV)
> [17] *After his return from the defeat of Chedorlaomer and the kings who were with him, the king of Sodom went out to meet him at the Valley of Shaveh (that is, the King's Valley).* [18] *And Melchizedek king of Salem brought out bread and wine. (He was priest of God Most High.)* [19] *And he blessed him and said, "Blessed be Abram by God Most High, Possessor of heaven and earth;* [20] *and blessed be God Most High, who has delivered your enemies into your hand!" And Abram gave him a tenth of everything.* [21] *And the king of Sodom said to Abram, "Give me the persons, but take the goods for yourself."* [22] *But Abram said to the king of Sodom, "I have lifted my hand to the LORD, God Most High, Possessor of heaven and earth,* [23] *that I would not take a thread or a sandal strap or anything that is yours, lest you should say, 'I have made Abram rich.'* [24] *I will take nothing but what the young men have eaten, and the share of the men who went with me. Let Aner, Eshcol, and Mamre take their share."*

Mysterious Melchizedek
Actually, Abram was met by two men. He was met by *Chedorlaomer* the king of Sodom, one of the alliance that was captured. Abram would receive no gift from him. Second, he was

met by Melchizedek, king of Salem (a first scriptural mention of ancient Jerusalem by that name), and a priest of the true God. From him, he gladly received bread and wine and a blessing. To him he gave a tenth of the spoils of war. In those early days, it was not unusual for a patriarch of a clan to serve as both priest and king. What is unique is that he was not a priest of an idolatrous religion, but worshipped the *Most High God*. Although not related genetically or historically to the called-out Hebrew people, here was one who somehow knew the true God.

Hebrews 7:1 (ESV)
[1] For this Melchizedek, king of Salem, priest of the Most High God, met Abraham returning from the slaughter of the kings and blessed him,

This and some other translations remind us that this was a bloody retaliation, by the fact they slaughtered the kings. If we only had the Genesis narrative, the mystique about Melchizedek would not be so great. However, he is brought up in other scriptures, each with inference to the Genesis passage and each adding mystery to him. For example, the entirety of Psalm 110 is a messianic chapter that includes this:

Psalm 110:4 (ESV)
[4] The LORD has sworn and will not change his mind, "You [implied Messiah] are a priest forever after the order of Melchizedek."

When we see messianic psalms like this, we recognize them as being highly prophetic. The Lord is giving us divine revelation about a then-future Messiah. He compares him to Melchizedek as being of the same priestly order.

Jesus Our Melchizedek
In the New Testament book of Hebrews, Melchizedek is mentioned by name eight times, but his priesthood as a type of Christ under the new covenant is the main theme from 4:14 through 10:18. Here is an excerpt:

Hebrews 6:19- 7:17 (ESV)
[19] We have this as a sure and steadfast anchor of the soul, a hope that enters into the inner place behind the curtain, [20] where Jesus has gone as a forerunner on our behalf, having become a high priest forever after the order of

Melchizedek. *¹ For this Melchizedek, king of Salem, priest of the Most High God, met Abraham returning from the slaughter of the kings and blessed him, ² and to him Abraham apportioned a tenth part of everything. He is first, by translation of his name, king of righteousness, and then he is also king of Salem, that is, king of peace. ³ He is without father or mother or genealogy, having neither beginning of days nor end of life, but resembling the Son of God he continues a priest forever. ⁴ See how great this man was to whom Abraham the patriarch gave a tenth of the spoils! ⁵ And those descendants of Levi who receive the priestly office have a commandment in the law to take tithes from the people, that is, from their brothers, though these also are descended from Abraham. ⁶ But this man who does not have his descent from them received tithes from Abraham and blessed him who had the promises. ⁷ It is beyond dispute that the inferior is blessed by the superior. ⁸ In the one case tithes are received by mortal men, but in the other case, by one of whom it is testified that he lives. ⁹ One might even say that Levi himself, who receives tithes, paid tithes through Abraham, ¹⁰ for he was still in the loins of his ancestor when Melchizedek met him. ¹¹ Now if perfection had been attainable through the Levitical priesthood (for under it the people received the law), what further need would there have been for another priest to arise after the order of Melchizedek, rather than one named after the order of Aaron? ¹² For when there is a change in the priesthood, there is necessarily a change in the law as well. ¹³ For the one of whom these things are spoken belonged to another tribe, from which no one has ever served at the altar. ¹⁴ For it is evident that our Lord was descended from Judah, and in connection with that tribe Moses said nothing about priests. ¹⁵ This becomes even more evident when another priest arises in the likeness of Melchizedek, ¹⁶ who has become a priest, not on the basis of a legal requirement concerning bodily descent, but by the power of an indestructible life. ¹⁷ For it is witnessed of him, "You are a priest forever, after the order of Melchizedek."*

Putting all of these passages together, and considering all that was said of Melchizedek, many theologians believe this was a christophany, that is, a pre-incarnate appearance of Christ. A synopsis supporting this view is given in verse 3. If so, it would be one of many such appearances, some of which later chapters of this book will consider. Others believe he was just a mortal to whom God revealed Himself. In my understanding he is indeed Christ himself. Verse 7 says *the inferior* [Abram] *was blessed by the superior* [Melchizedek]. It is hard to imagine any mere mortal greater before God than Abram. Then verse 8 says that Levitical priests who collect tithes ultimately die, but Melchizedek who was paid a tithe by Abraham is still living. It seems the Hebrews writer was leading us to identify Melchizedek with Jesus.

What we do want to take away from this passage is that just as Melchizedek was a high priest to Abram, Jesus is our high priest under the new covenant. At the very least, he was a type, a prefiguring, of Christ. Perhaps this is what Jesus was reflecting upon when he said, *"Your father Abraham rejoiced to see My day, and he saw it and was glad."* The fact that Abram paid tithes to this man who he had never before met shows that he regarded him as having a divine connection, as being a divine representative. His tithe was an act of worship. As Abram did before Melchizedek, he was doing by faith before Christ. If Abram, who lived long before Jesus, had messianic faith, how much more should we have faith in our great high priest--we who have not only the witness of the Spirit, but also the witness of history to reaffirm the scriptural promise of redemption for sinners.

Beyond faith in this identity is the promise of God's presence and favor. The context and tenor of these reference verses is entirely priestly in nature. It emphasizes Jesus as our advocate before the very throne of heaven. God has provided us a tangible and authoritative demonstration of his favor in giving us Jesus, our Great High Priest. This is the real sanctuary – the heavenly one. It is equivalent in priority to having our name written in the Lamb's book of life.

In the book of Hebrews, all this is set in contrast with the priesthood under the Law of Moses. Under the law, only those descended from Levi could serve as priests. However, as was Melchizedek, so is Jesus after the same order, and not of the Levitical lineage, our Great High Priest. Since he is in that position based on *the power of an indestructible life*, then our salvation is more secure than a strong fortress. It is as secure as that indestructible life.

Abraham's encounter with the king and priest of Salem was a significant event, a divine appointment. Melchizedek came out to bless Abram for having conquered the alliance of kings that had captured Lot and many people. Here to Abram was revealed the priestly role of Messiah. This priestly messianic role is not his most dominant role in the Old Testament, but it is perhaps the oldest. It is rooted and introduced here, and it is critical in the economy of the New Covenant. No doubt, much of the apostolic perception of Jesus' high priestly role, as conveyed to us in the New Testament, was founded on this encounter.

The complete dynamics of what was done and said on that day remains sketchy. We have only a couple of brief statements by Melchizedek, and Abram's only reported statements were to the king of Sodom who also came to meet him, but nothing to Melchizedek. Yet we can imagine the interchange was much more extensive than that. No doubt, as Abram paid tithes to Melchizedek, he spoke words of reverence and praise to God and to him. We can only speculate on the extent of Abram's vision on this episode. He understood enough that he was instantly motivated to worship by giving a tenth of the spoils to him. How much did he understand? Did he realize the messianic overtones? Did he recognize the divine nature? I believe he knew something of these truths. Regardless, we don't have to speculate to allow its full implication to speak to us. May we join with Abram in celebrating the grace of God for his great High Priest.

Jesus Has the Position to Be Our High Priest
We have been considering the high-priestly role of Jesus. A prevalent aspect of that is the fact that Jesus in his glorified state sat down at the Father's right hand. After his ascension, Mark's gospel tells us this:

Mark 16:19 (ESV)
[19] So then the Lord Jesus, after he had spoken to them, was taken up into heaven and sat down at the right hand of God.

This idea is repeated often in scripture regarding Jesus' role. His position at the right hand of the Almighty stresses his preeminence and his divine authority.

Hebrews 8:1-6 (NIV2011)
[1] Now the main point of what we are saying is this: We do have such a high priest, who sat down at the right hand of the throne of the Majesty in heaven, [2] and who serves in the

sanctuary, the true tabernacle set up by the Lord, not by a mere human being.

Jesus considered it an integral testimony about who he was when he testified before the Sanhedrin.

> *Matthew 26:62-64 (ESV)*
> *[62] And the high priest stood up and said, "Have you no answer to make? What is it that these men testify against you?" [63] But Jesus remained silent. And the high priest said to him, "I adjure you by the living God, tell us if you are the Christ, the Son of God." [64] Jesus said to him, "You have said so. But I tell you, from now on you will see the Son of Man seated at the right hand of Power and coming on the clouds of heaven."*

Earlier, Jesus was contending with the religious leaders over his own identity and role. He quoted from Psalm 110:1 and questioned them over it. They could not answer him.

> *Mark 12:35-36 (ESV)*
> *[35] And as Jesus taught in the temple, he said, "How can the scribes say that the Christ is the son of David? [36] David himself, in the Holy Spirit, declared, "'The Lord said to my Lord, "Sit at my right hand, until I put your enemies under your feet."'*

Jesus was not being promoted to a brand new level of glory when he sat down at God's right hand. He was being restored to his rightful place, as reflected in his prayer just prior to his crucifixion and resurrection.

> *John 17:5 (NKJV)*
> *[5] And now, O Father, glorify Me together with Yourself, with the glory which I had with You before the world was.*

The apostles clearly grasped this message and passed it on in their teaching to the early church and to listening outsiders. On Pentecost, they told the Jews looking on what was happening.

> *Acts 2:33-35 (ESV)*
> *[33] Being therefore exalted at the right hand of God, and having received from the Father the promise of the Holy Spirit, he has poured out this that you yourselves are seeing*

and hearing. ³⁴ For David did not ascend into the heavens, but he himself says, "'The Lord said to my Lord, "Sit at my right hand, ³⁵ until I make your enemies your footstool."'

Shortly afterwards, standing before the same religious leaders that had heard Jesus' testimony about himself sitting beside God the Father, they too taught that same message. They were pronouncing judgment upon the leaders by so doing.

Acts 5:30-35 (ESV)
³⁰ The God of our fathers raised Jesus, whom you killed by hanging him on a tree. ³¹ God exalted him at his right hand as Leader and Savior, to give repentance to Israel and forgiveness of sins. ³² And we are witnesses to these things, and so is the Holy Spirit, whom God has given to those who obey him."

The significance of this position of Jesus at God's right hand was promoted by Paul after his conversion, as seen in his letter to the church at Ephesus.

Ephesians 1:19-20 (ESV)
¹⁹ and what is the immeasurable greatness of his power toward us who believe, according to the working of his great might ²⁰ that he worked in Christ when he raised him from the dead and seated him at his right hand in the heavenly places,

Peter connected Jesus' great authority with his being seated at God's right hand.

1 Peter 3:22 (ESV)
²² [Jesus] who has gone into heaven and is at the right hand of God, with angels, authorities, and powers having been subjected to him.

The author of Hebrews, summarizing the infinite extent of Jesus' power and glory, includes that same concept in concluding the nature of Christ. Then he repeats it later in his letter.

Hebrews 1:3 (ESV)
³ He is the radiance of the glory of God and the exact

imprint of his nature, and he upholds the universe by the word of his power. After making purification for sins, he sat down at the right hand of the Majesty on high,

Hebrews 10:12 (ESV)
12 But when Christ had offered for all time a single sacrifice for sins, he sat down at the right hand of God,

Jesus Has the Credentials to Serve as High Priest

The writer of Hebrews summarizes two main ideas in the following passage concerning the adequacy of being a priest, any priest.

Hebrews 5:1-10 (NIV2011)
1 Every high priest is selected from among the people and is appointed to represent the people in matters related to God, to offer gifts and sacrifices for sins. 2 He is able to deal gently with those who are ignorant and are going astray, since he himself is subject to weakness. 3 This is why he has to offer sacrifices for his own sins, as well as for the sins of the people. 4 And no one takes this honor on himself, but he receives it when called by God, just as Aaron was. 5 In the same way, Christ did not take on himself the glory of becoming a high priest. But God said to him, "You are my Son; today I have become your Father." 6 And he says in another place, "You are a priest forever, in the order of Melchizedek." 7 During the days of Jesus' life on earth, he offered up prayers and petitions with fervent cries and tears to the one who could save him from death, and he was heard because of his reverent submission. 8 Son though he was, he learned obedience from what he suffered 9 and, once made perfect, he became the source of eternal salvation for all who obey him 10 and was designated by God to be high priest in the order of Melchizedek.

The two big concepts the writer wants us to see are, first, the priest must identify with those being represented by him before God. He must be of their same nature. He must be able to deal sympathetically and gently with them.

Hebrews 4:15 (ESV)
15 For we do not have a high priest who is unable to sympathize with our weaknesses, but one who in every respect has been tempted as we are, yet without sin.

> *Hebrews 2:14-18 (NIV2011)*
> *[14] Since the children have flesh and blood, he too shared in their humanity so that by his death he might break the power of him who holds the power of death—that is, the devil— [15] and free those who all their lives were held in slavery by their fear of death. [16] For surely it is not angels he helps, but Abraham's descendants. [17] For this reason he had to be made like them, fully human in every way, in order that he might become a merciful and faithful high priest in service to God, and that he might make atonement for the sins of the people. [18] Because he himself suffered when he was tempted, he is able to help those who are being tempted.*

Second, he wants us to understand that the priesthood is not acquired through aspiration or training. It is granted by God's purpose. Priests under the Levitical priesthood inherited it only by being of the family of Aaron, within the tribe of Levi. Likewise, Jesus did not seek the role of high priest and receive it as a favor. The Father made him a priest, as purposed and stated in anticipation centuries before, and embodied symbolically in our episode between Abram and Melchizedek.

Because we have a sympathetic and faithful high priest:

> *Hebrews 4:16 (NIV2011)*
> *[16] Let us then approach God's throne of grace with confidence, so that we may receive mercy and find grace to help us in our time of need.*

Another credential for the acceptable priesthood of the new covenant is mentioned repeatedly in the book of Hebrews and elsewhere. It is the need for an enduring priesthood. The phrase that he is *a priest forever* is one of the most often quoted Old Testament phrases in the New Testament as well as elsewhere in the Old Testament. This alone underscores its significance to Christians today.

> *Hebrews 7:21-27 (ESV)*
> *[21] but this one was made a priest with an oath by the one who said to him: "The Lord has sworn and will not change his mind, 'You are a priest forever.'" [22] This makes Jesus the guarantor of a better covenant. [23] The former priests were many in number, because they were prevented by*

death from continuing in office, ^{24} but he holds his priesthood permanently, because he continues forever. ^{25} Consequently, he is able to save to the uttermost those who draw near to God through him, since he always lives to make intercession for them. ^{26} For it was indeed fitting that we should have such a high priest, holy, innocent, unstained, separated from sinners, and exalted above the heavens. ^{27} He has no need, like those high priests, to offer sacrifices daily, first for his own sins and then for those of the people, since he did this once for all when he offered up himself.

Jesus Our High Priest Brought a Worthy Sacrifice

Hebrews 8:3 (ESV)
^{3} For every high priest is appointed to offer gifts and sacrifices; thus it is necessary for this priest also to have something to offer.

Under the Levitical priesthood, the high priest did not enter the inner sanctuary empty-handed on the annual Day of Atonement. He entered with blood from a sacrificed animal, offered as substitute for the person bringing it. All that was just a foreshadow of Jesus' as our Great High Priest having entered the heavenly sanctuary with his own blood as testimony of our repentance and seeking mercy. This is the current status of the atoning process, while we anticipate his enemies eventually being brought under his authority.

Hebrews 10:13-14 (ESV)
^{13} waiting from that time until his enemies should be made a footstool for his feet. ^{14} For by a single offering he has perfected for all time those who are being sanctified.

Hebrews 9:11-12 (ESV)
^{11} But when Christ appeared as a high priest of the good things that have come, then through the greater and more perfect tent (not made with hands, that is, not of this creation) ^{12} he entered once for all into the holy places, not by means of the blood of goats and calves but by means of his own blood, thus securing an eternal redemption.

Jesus' sacrifice of himself is our eternally worthy offering before the throne of glory, the throne of grace, he who orchestrated all of this.

Jesus' Intercessory Role as High Priest

In the most illustrative Old Testament portrait of the Messiah in his suffering servant role, Isaiah chapter 53, he ends with a snapshot of the priestly Messiah. It gives a preview of what his activity would include.

> *Isaiah 53:12 (ESV)*
> *[12] Therefore I will divide him a portion with the many, and he shall divide the spoil with the strong, because he poured out his soul to death and was numbered with the transgressors; yet he bore the sin of many, and makes intercession for the transgressors.*

That last phrase prefigures his priestly role, set along with his suffering servant role. Intercession would be a part of what he does on an ongoing basis, so long as we are being sanctified during this present life. We know we are weak and vulnerable in our own power. We know also that we have an enemy who is our accuser before God. But we have this promise based on our faithful High Priest:

> *Romans 8:33-34 (ESV)*
> *[33] Who shall bring any charge against God's elect? It is God who justifies. [34] Who is to condemn? Christ Jesus is the one who died—more than that, who was raised—who is at the right hand of God, who indeed is interceding for us.*

> *Hebrews 7:25 (ESV)*
> *[25] Consequently, he is able to save to the uttermost those who draw near to God through him, since he always lives to make intercession for them.*

We can see how Jesus' intercession sanctifies us before God. But how does that intercession affect our daily walk with the Lord? How does his intercession guide our actions? Luke recounts how Peter and the other apostles taught the crowds in Jerusalem on the day of Pentecost, following the baptism of the Holy Spirit. Jesus, from his position as our High Priest, began dispensing the promised Comforter.

> *Acts 2:31-33 (NIV2011)*
> *[31] Seeing what was to come, he spoke of the resurrection of the Messiah, that he was not abandoned to the realm of the*

dead, nor did his body see decay. ³² God has raised this Jesus to life, and we are all witnesses of it. ³³ Exalted to the right hand of God, he has received from the Father the promised Holy Spirit and has poured out what you now see and hear.

Some time later Paul wrote about the astonishing role of the Holy Spirit in our prayer life.

Romans 8:26-27 (ESV)
²⁶ Likewise the Spirit helps us in our weakness. For we do not know what to pray for as we ought, but the Spirit himself intercedes for us with groanings too deep for words. ²⁷ And he who searches hearts knows what is the mind of the Spirit, because the Spirit intercedes for the saints according to the will of God.

Here we read that the Holy Spirit intercedes for us. *And he who searches hearts,* Jesus (Heb 4:12, Rev 2:23) is interceding. All three members of the divine Trinity are actively involved when we pray, especially since we do not always know God's will and do not know what to pray.

Thus, the Holy Spirit is active in the intercessory priesthood of Jesus. This reminds us that our prayers are personal and spiritual before God, not just a legal formula. A spiritual relationship is in view here. He loves us and Jesus loves us.

John 17:9-10 (NKJV)
⁹ I pray for them [the disciples]. *I do not pray for the world but for those whom You have given Me, for they are Yours. ¹⁰ And all Mine are Yours, and Yours are Mine, and I am glorified in them.*

In case we might be inclined to apply Jesus' expressions of love in John 17 just to the twelve, or just to those believers present during his sin-bearing, Jesus gave us this assurance:

John 17:20-21 (NKJV)
²⁰ "I do not pray for these alone, but also for those who will believe in Me through their word; ²¹ that they all may be one, as You, Father, are in Me, and I in You; that they also may be one in Us, that the world may believe that You sent Me.

Our High Priest Enfolds Us in Divine Fellowship
The work of our High Priest might be summarized in the concept of developing a vital and fitting relationship between ourselves and the Lord. That relationship cannot be fully described by statements of truth. The Lord himself regularly spoke of it using terms of endearment. For an excellent example of this, read the entire seventeenth chapter of John's gospel, Jesus' high-priestly prayer in the upper room just before his arrest. Here is a verse from that prayer.

> *John 17:13 (NKJV)*
> [13] *But now I* [Jesus] *come to You* [The Father], *and these things I speak in the world, that they* [his disciples] *may have My joy fulfilled in themselves.*

Later John wrote this in a letter, expressing the same undiminished relational passion:

> *1 John 1:3-4 (NKJV)*
> [3] *that which we have seen and heard we declare to you, that you also may have fellowship with us; and truly our fellowship is with the Father and with His Son Jesus Christ.*
> [4] *And these things we write to you that your joy may be full.*

Jesus had previously predicted the sending of the Spirit to his church, his bride.

> *John 14:16-18 (NKJV)*
> [16] *And I will pray the Father, and He will give you another Helper, that He may abide with you forever--* [17] *the Spirit of truth, whom the world cannot receive, because it neither sees Him nor knows Him; but you know Him, for He dwells with you and will be in you.* [18] *I will not leave you orphans; I will come to you.*

He would not leave them as orphans. He anticipated their sense of futile devastation after his death. He was reassuring them that he had not finished caring for them. He would not leave them as orphans. He would not leave them helpless to fend for themselves. In his high priestly role, he would come to them in the person of the Holy Spirit. *I will come to you,* the last phrase of verse 18, is speaking of that coming of the Spirit. The writer of Hebrews tells the basis for the security of this promise.

> *Hebrews 6:19-20a (NIV2011)*
> *[19] We have this hope as an anchor for the soul, firm and secure. It enters the inner sanctuary behind the curtain, [20] where our forerunner, Jesus, has entered on our behalf...*

Our hope is anchored by Jesus in the heavenly throne room where he has already preceded us and makes intercession for us. Furthermore, he sidesteps all barriers to our fellowship with the Divine Presence. Even while he was still walking this earth, Jesus revealed his predisposition to share in fellowship with his followers, revealing his glory to them.

> *John 17:24-25 (ESV)*
> *[24] Father, I desire that they also, whom you have given me, may be with me where I am, to see my glory that you have given me because you loved me before the foundation of the world. [25] O righteous Father, even though the world does not know you, I know you, and these know that you have sent me.*

Jesus articulates his intimate love for the Father, then immediately ties his desire of enfolding his followers into that intimacy.

To underscore the personal and intimate nature of the fellowship, that Jesus predestined to implement with his disciples, look at the following excerpt from the book of Acts. It is a historical account of the execution of Stephen. He had stood before the Jewish people and their leaders and told them the truth about Jesus. They didn't want to hear it. As he was facing death, he was given a vision by the Holy Spirit in which he saw a snapshot into heaven. He saw the glory of God. He also saw Jesus standing at the right hand of the Father.

> *Acts 7:54-56 (ESV)*
> *[54] Now when they heard these things they were enraged, and they ground their teeth at him. [55] But he, full of the Holy Spirit, gazed into heaven and saw the glory of God, and Jesus standing at the right hand of God. [56] And he said, "Behold, I see the heavens opened, and the Son of Man standing at the right hand of God."*

If you read the rest of the story, you see that this proclaimed vision so antagonized the leaders that they drug him out of the city and stoned him to death. There are many implications we could discuss about this episode but I want to focus on one small detail. In many other passages, we have read that Jesus is seated at God's right hand as he administers his high-priestly role. In this narrative, Steven saw Jesus standing beside God's right hand, not sitting. In this intense circumstance, it seems that Jesus has risen from his seat of honor and power to more personally participate in Steven's sacrificial death. Perhaps he arose to welcome him; certainly to take close and caring note of it.

The result of Jesus' priestly role is an endearing, intimate, personal relationship which extends into eternity.

Our High Priest Sanctifies Us
Jesus is active in his high priestly role. He is not only the source and means of our justification, he is also busily involved in our growth. Besides interceding for us and besides drawing us into fellowship with God, he also is busy in sanctifying us. Our Hebrews author states it this way.

> *Hebrews 12:2 (NKJV)*
> *² looking unto Jesus, the author and finisher of our faith, who for the joy that was set before Him endured the cross, despising the shame, and has sat down at the right hand of the throne of God.*

In addition to being our Savior, Jesus is the *finisher* or perfecter of our faith. Through the empowering and guiding of the Holy Spirit, he is working in our individual lives to accomplish a specific goal.

> *Romans 8:9-11 (NKJV)*
> *⁹ But you are not in the flesh but in the Spirit, if indeed the Spirit of God dwells in you. Now if anyone does not have the Spirit of Christ, he is not His. ¹⁰ And if Christ is in you, the body is dead because of sin, but the Spirit is life because of righteousness. ¹¹ But if the Spirit of Him who raised Jesus from the dead dwells in you, He who raised Christ from the dead will also give life to your mortal bodies through His Spirit who dwells in you.*

Note in this passage that the Holy Spirit is referred to as *the Spirit, the Spirit of God,* and *the Spirit of Christ* without fear of confusion.

> *Romans 8:29 (ESV)*
> *²⁹ For those whom he foreknew he also predestined to be conformed to the image of his Son, in order that he might be the firstborn among many brothers.*

That one specific summary goal toward which we are being aimed is summed up in this passage; to be like Christ in his character attributes. Striving toward that goal, we share in a brotherhood with him in the presence of the Father. How astounding, how incredible, how staggering is that, *that he might be the firstborn among many brothers*!

> *Romans 12:2 (ESV)*
> *² Do not be conformed to this world, but be transformed by the renewal of your mind, that by testing you may discern what is the will of God, what is good and acceptable and perfect.*

Thus, we can set our sights on perfection so that our objective is always in sight. Sanctification is summarized by the process of our growing toward the character of Christ.

Sanctification is advanced through the application of God's truth to our lives. The way we learn His truth is through His word, the Holy Scriptures. Yet for us to fully comprehend and apply the truths of scripture requires another function of Christ's high-priestly role. We need the Holy Spirit to supernaturally interpret and magnify those scriptures in the eyes of our hearts.

> *Ephesians 1:16-19 (ESV)*
> *¹⁶ I do not cease to give thanks for you, remembering you in my prayers, ¹⁷ that the God of our Lord Jesus Christ, the Father of glory, may give you the Spirit of wisdom and of revelation in the knowledge of him, ¹⁸ having the eyes of your hearts enlightened, that you may know what is the hope to which he has called you, what are the riches of his glorious inheritance in the saints, ¹⁹ and what is the immeasurable greatness of his power toward us who believe, according to the working of his great might*

> *Colossians 1:9-10 (ESV)*
> *⁹ And so, from the day we heard, we have not ceased to pray for you, asking that you may be filled with the knowledge of*

his will in all spiritual wisdom and understanding, ^{10} so as to walk in a manner worthy of the Lord, fully pleasing to him, bearing fruit in every good work and increasing in the knowledge of God.

Our High Priest leads us to understanding and wisdom in interpreting scripture. The Holy Spirit is his agent of change. He gives vitality, bringing them to life in our minds.

Isaiah 55:10-11 (NKJV)
^{10} "For as the rain comes down, and the snow from heaven, And do not return there, But water the earth, And make it bring forth and bud, That it may give seed to the sower And bread to the eater, ^{11} So shall My word be that goes forth from My mouth; It shall not return to Me void, But it shall accomplish what I please, And it shall prosper in the thing for which I sent it.

Hebrews 4:12 (ESV)
^{12} For the word of God is living and active, sharper than any two-edged sword, piercing to the division of soul and of spirit, of joints and of marrow, and discerning the thoughts and intentions of the heart.

2 Timothy 3:15 (ESV)
^{15} and how from childhood you have been acquainted with the sacred writings, which are able to make you wise for salvation through faith in Christ Jesus.

God caused past events and letters to be written down and preserved so that we could attain the knowledge promised under the new covenant. Repeating two passages quoted in the Preface:

Romans 15:4 (NKJV)
^{4} For whatever things were written before were written for our learning, that we through the patience and comfort of the Scriptures might have hope.

1 Corinthians 10:11 (NKJV)
^{11} Now all these things happened to them as examples, and they were written for our admonition, upon whom the ends of the ages have come.

Our Great High Priest facilitates this work of the Spirit in translating written words on a page into living guidelines for hope and joy.

Finally, our sanctification is channeled into marching orders. Jesus prayed this to the Father in the hearing of the disciples on the night he was betrayed.

> *John 17:18-19 (NKJV)*
> *[18] As You sent Me into the world, I also have sent them into the world. [19] And for their sakes I sanctify Myself, that they also may be sanctified by the truth.*

A Royal Priesthood

The concept of a priesthood did not originate with Abram, but it was confirmed to him as we have been discussing. Much later the tribe of Levi was designated by God through Moses to be the priestly tribe. Under Mosaic law, no one could act the part of a formal priest except the Levites. Yet, in that same period, God told this to Moses.

> *Exodus 19:5-6 (ESV)*
> *[5] Now therefore, if you will indeed obey my voice and keep my covenant, you shall be my treasured possession among all peoples, for all the earth is mine; [6] and you shall be to me a kingdom of priests and a holy nation. These are the words that you shall speak to the people of Israel."*

How could the people at large be a kingdom of priests? While they were not allowed to carry out formal priestly duties such as animal sacrifice and incense burning, the people were to be priests in some sense. They were to serve God in their daily lives and make known the knowledge of Him to all people, striving to live a life of holiness, as He is holy.

This same calling was applied to the New Testament church by the apostolic writers. Speaking to the church, and quoting Old Testament phrases, they wrote:

> *1 Peter 2:9 (ESV)*
> *[9] But you are a chosen race, a royal priesthood, a holy nation, a people for his own possession, that you may proclaim the excellencies of him who called you out of darkness into his marvelous light.*

2 Timothy 1:9 (ESV)
⁹ who saved us and called us to a holy calling, not because of our works but because of his own purpose and grace, which he gave us in Christ Jesus before the ages began,

Titus 2:14 (ESV)
¹⁴ who gave himself for us to redeem us from all lawlessness and to purify for himself a people for his own possession who are zealous for good works.

Revelation 5:10 (ESV)
¹⁰ and you have made them a kingdom and priests to our God, and they shall reign on the earth."

The same purposes originally given to the Jews, but later temporarily taken away, are now given to followers of Jesus. All this is foreshadowed in the person of Melchizedek, and shown to Abram. This patriarchal vision still speaks to us. God is showing us His big idea, lest we see this as just a curious ancient isolated story. The redemptive messianic thread runs throughout the tapestry of biblical time. As followers of Jesus, behold! --we have now been consecrated a *royal priesthood*, a *holy nation, the Lord's own possession*. We should strive to live holy lives so that our conduct might testify to the world about our glorious God, as we serve as a royal priesthood. And consider that we—even we—are considered by God as His treasured possession. How profound is that? What a grand and glorious calling it is!

Chapter 3
The Unthinkable Test

The Narrative
Now we come to a passage in Genesis that is one of the more commonly known stories of the Bible and is possibly the most emotionally intense story in the Old Testament. It conjures up a personal protest from within the reader, crying, "NO! You can't possibly mean that." It isn't pleasant reading. Please keep reading anyway, because I believe this story will lead us into a truth about God Himself that is most remarkable.

> *Genesis 22:1-14 (ESV)*
> *¹ After these things God tested Abraham and said to him, "Abraham!" And he said, "Here I am." ² He said, "Take your son, your only son Isaac, whom you love, and go to the land of Moriah, and offer him there as a burnt offering on one of the mountains of which I shall tell you." ³ So Abraham rose early in the morning, saddled his donkey, and took two of his young men with him, and his son Isaac. And he cut the wood for the burnt offering and arose and went to the place of which God had told him. ⁴ On the third day Abraham lifted up his eyes and saw the place from afar. ⁵ Then Abraham said to his young men, "Stay here with the donkey; I and the boy will go over there and worship and come again to you." ⁶ And Abraham took the wood of the burnt offering and laid it on Isaac his son. And he took in his hand the fire and the knife. So they went both of them together. ⁷ And Isaac said to his father Abraham, "My father!" And he said, "Here I am, my son." He said, "Behold, the fire and the wood, but where is the lamb for a burnt offering?" ⁸ Abraham said, "God will provide for himself the lamb for a burnt offering, my son." So they went both of them together. ⁹ When they came to the place of which God had told him, Abraham built the altar there and laid the wood in order and bound Isaac his son and laid him on the altar, on top of the wood. ¹⁰ Then Abraham reached out his hand and took the knife to slaughter his son. ¹¹ But the angel of the LORD called to him from heaven and said,*

> *"Abraham, Abraham!" And he said, "Here I am."* [12] *He said, "Do not lay your hand on the boy or do anything to him, for now I know that you fear God, seeing you have not withheld your son, your only son, from me."* [13] *And Abraham lifted up his eyes and looked, and behold, behind him was a ram, caught in a thicket by his horns. And Abraham went and took the ram and offered it up as a burnt offering instead of his son.* [14] *So Abraham called the name of that place, "The LORD will provide"; as it is said to this day, "On the mount of the LORD it shall be provided."*

I mentioned that this is an emotionally intense passage. When we read it, we want to cry out, "No!" The requirement is unthinkable. Yet, where is the emotion? Nothing is said in the narrative about Abraham's feelings, his heart, his thoughts. It is a rather objective statement of events. We almost get the impression that Abraham is a mechanically obedient robot of a man who holds no passions. To read this is almost a numbing of our sensitivities. If this were being written in western novel style, the story would be heavily draped with vivid expressions of agonizing struggle. Abraham's anguish would be detailed for the reader. Nothing would be left for the imagination.

When Moses wrote this, he was writing to a very different culture. They were probably a more right-brain people than most of us. They had no problem reading between the lines to understand the passionate groping going on in Abraham's mind. It was normal for them to supply the missing emotion. A lot of Hebrew narrative is written in this manner. Emotion is never mentioned, only the historical facts. The Hebrew reader is left to supply the assumed emotions. Thus, we shall assume that Abraham was a man having normal emotions. So let's call on the right side of our brain to fully experience the emotion of this story which will be key to grasping the grand message of the narrative. We will investigate Abraham's assumed emotions in this chapter.

A Message of a Different Kind
When hearing this narrative taught and making application to our lives, the main point is typically to see this sacrificing faith of Abraham as a model for our own faith. We are called to emulate it. Abraham was certainly commended for it.

> *Genesis 22:15-18 (ESV)*
> [15] *And the angel of the LORD called to Abraham a second*

> *time from heaven* [16] *and said, "By myself I have sworn, declares the LORD, because you have done this and have not withheld your son, your only son,* [17] *I will surely bless you, and I will surely multiply your offspring as the stars of heaven and as the sand that is on the seashore. And your offspring shall possess the gate of his enemies,* [18] *and in your offspring shall all the nations of the earth be blessed, because you have obeyed my voice."*

And in the New Testament, James used this very account as an object lesson for genuine faith.

> *James 2:20-23 (NIV2011)*
> [20] *You foolish person, do you want evidence that faith without deeds is useless?* [21] *Was not our father Abraham considered righteous for what he did when he offered his son Isaac on the altar?* [22] *You see that his faith and his actions were working together, and his faith was made complete by what he did.* [23] *And the scripture was fulfilled that says, "Abraham believed God, and it was credited to him as righteousness," and he was called God's friend.*

Even in reading the narrative privately, it is difficult to not put ourselves in Abraham's place and ask, "Would I be able to do that?" For most of us, the answer is troubling, regardless of how we answered. That is what makes this hard to read. If that is your perspective, then this is probably not one of your favorite passages for meditation.

But I suggest that another message--a different message--may be gained from the passage. We will suggest a different purpose and application than simply unquestioning faith. Instead of trying to make this a test of our emotions and decisions, we will keep the test on Abraham, and see God revealing something wonderful to us about Himself. This exploration will be powerful!

Examining the Passage
God's instruction in this passage starts out strangely. He calls Abraham to sacrifice *your son, your only Son—Isaac*. This phrase is repeated by God. If you are familiar with the story, you know that Abraham had another son, Ishmael, who was thirteen years older than Isaac. Ishmael was Abraham's firstborn. Yet God made a point to intentionally call Isaac his *only son*. Why is that?

When Abraham and Sarah grew impatient after waiting over ten years to have a child as God had promised, they tried in their own scheme to have a child through a surrogate wife, Sarah's handmaid Hagar. Hagar, an Egyptian, bore a son, Ishmael. But Ishmael was not God's intended heir to the messianic lineage, not the covenant son God had promised.

> *Genesis 17:15-22 (ESV)*
> *[15] And God said to Abraham, "As for Sarai your wife, you shall not call her name Sarai, but Sarah shall be her name. [16] I will bless her, and moreover, I will give you a son by her. I will bless her, and she shall become nations; kings of peoples shall come from her." [17] Then Abraham fell on his face and laughed and said to himself, "Shall a child be born to a man who is a hundred years old? Shall Sarah, who is ninety years old, bear a child?" [18] And Abraham said to God, "Oh that Ishmael might live before you!" [19] God said, "No, but Sarah your wife shall bear you a son, and you shall call his name Isaac. I will establish my covenant with him as an everlasting covenant for his offspring after him. [20] As for Ishmael, I have heard you; behold, I have blessed him and will make him fruitful and multiply him greatly. He shall father twelve princes, and I will make him into a great nation. [21] But I will establish my covenant with Isaac, whom Sarah shall bear to you at this time next year." [22] When he had finished talking with him, God went up from Abraham.*

Thus, Isaac, though not Abraham's first biological son, was the *only son* of the covenant, who would continue the messianic lineage that would eventually give birth to Messiah.

Next, note the place where God commanded Abraham to go to make this sacrifice.

> *Genesis 22:2 (NIV2011)*
> *[2] Then God said, "Take your son, your only son, whom you love—Isaac—and go to the region of Moriah. Sacrifice him there as a burnt offering on a mountain I will show you."*

The name Moriah is only used twice in scripture, here and in the following passage that identifies its location for us.

> *2 Chronicles 3:1 (NIV2011)*
> *[1] Then Solomon began to build the temple of the LORD in*

> Jerusalem on Mount Moriah, where the LORD had appeared to his father David. It was on the threshing floor of Araunah the Jebusite, the place provided by David.

This identity will become significant as we develop its importance following. In short, it is a specific mountain that would someday be enclosed within the city of Jerusalem.

Isaac Was a Type

The command and obedience of Abraham in this narrative was something more than a test of his faith, although it certainly was that. But its significance doesn't end there. In this narrative, Isaac stands as a type of something. A "type" is a person that is a symbolic prediction of a later, greater person. The near-sacrifice of Isaac speaks to us prophetically of the real Lamb of God that would be sacrificed for the sins of the world in the distant future. It is a picture of Jesus being crucified. How do we make this connection? God has provided us several parallel elements in the narrative to link the two stories together. Let's look at them.

Covenant Sons

First of all, Isaac was Abraham's covenant son, as we have already discussed. He was Abraham's *only son* of the messianic heritage. Likewise, Jesus is the Son of the new covenant, as attested to in these verses.

> *Jeremiah 31:31 (NIV2011)*
> *31 "The days are coming," declares the LORD, "when I will make a new covenant with the people of Israel and with the people of Judah.*

> *John 1:29 (NIV2011)*
> *29 The next day John saw Jesus coming toward him and said, "Look, the Lamb of God, who takes away the sin of the world!*

> *Luke 22:20 (NIV2011)*
> *20 In the same way, after the supper he took the cup, saying, "This cup is the new covenant in my blood, which is poured out for you.*

> *Hebrews 8:6 (NIV2011)*
> *6 But in fact the ministry Jesus has received is as superior to theirs as the covenant of which he is mediator is superior*

to the old one, since the new covenant is established on better promises.

Hebrews 9:15 (NIV2011)
15 For this reason Christ is the mediator of a new covenant, that those who are called may receive the promised eternal inheritance—now that he has died as a ransom to set them free from the sins committed under the first covenant.

Hebrews 12:23-24 (NIV2011)
23 ... You have come ... 24 to Jesus the mediator of a new covenant, and to the sprinkled blood that speaks a better word than the blood of Abel.

Both Isaac and Jesus were the one and only sons of their respective covenant. Isaac was the son of the old covenant; Jesus was the Son of the new covenant.

The Mountain
Isaac made the three-day journey from the desert to the Judean mountains. He accompanied his father Abraham to a specific mountain: Moriah, where he was prepared for sacrifice. In the same way, Jesus was led up a mountain, called Golgotha in New Testament times, to be prepared for sacrifice. That mountain on which Jesus was sacrificed was geographically the same mountain region to which Isaac had traveled. The actual temple mount in Jerusalem is identified as Moriah. This was where sacrifices for sin were made and is symbolically the sacrificial mount. The true sacrificial mount, Golgotha hill, on which Jesus was crucified, was near to the temple mount, but was located outside the city wall. It likely is the same range of hills as that inside the wall. Thus, out of all the mountains in Judea, both Isaac and Jesus were brought for sacrifice to the same location!

The Burdens
Just as Isaac carried the wood on his back from the place where the donkey and servants were left behind to the sacrificial mount, so Jesus likewise bore his cross on the way to that spot. Both carried their own wooden implements of death.

Submission
Isaac is now a young man. He probably could have won a wrestling match with his father and certainly could have won in a foot race to escape. Yet, he did not resist when Abraham bound

him and laid him on the altar. Likewise, Jesus did not resist his executioners. As Isaiah prophesied, our Savior did not protest.

Isaiah 53:7 (NIV2011)
⁷ He was oppressed and afflicted, yet he did not open his mouth; he was led like a lamb to the slaughter, and as a sheep before its shearers is silent, so he did not open his mouth.

In this, Isaac was a worthy type of Christ.

Abandoned
When Abraham and Isaac came within sight of mount Moriah, they stopped, left the donkey there with his two young servants, and only he and the boy went to the mountain of sacrifice. Had the servants been with them, they would undoubtedly have tried to prevent Abraham from carrying out God's command. As it was, no one was available to help, or rescue Isaac from this destiny. In the same way, Jesus was alone in his arrest in the Garden of Gethsemane. His apostles scattered. They fled to avoid capture. Peter later denied him. Jesus bore the cross alone.

Matthew 26:56 (NIV2011)
⁵⁶ But this has all taken place that the writings of the prophets might be fulfilled." Then all the disciples deserted him and fled.

A Substitute Offered
In the narrative on Isaac's near-sacrifice, God halted his execution and provided a ram caught in the thicket by its horns as a substitute sacrifice. In the trial of Jesus before Pontius Pilate, we also find a substitute was offered for him. Pilate desired to let Jesus go free. Yet, Pilate was held hostage, so to speak, by the Jewish leaders who posed a threat to report him to Caesar as being soft on a treasonous rebel if he would not crucify Jesus. Here is the account.

Matthew 27:15-18 (NIV2011)
¹⁵ Now it was the governor's custom at the festival to release a prisoner chosen by the crowd. ¹⁶ At that time they had a well-known prisoner whose name was Jesus Barabbas. ¹⁷ So when the crowd had gathered, Pilate asked them, "Which one do you want me to release to you: Jesus Barabbas, or Jesus who is called the Messiah?" ¹⁸ For he

knew it was out of self-interest that they had handed Jesus over to him.

Pilate decided to exercise his custom to release a prisoner to the people. In this way, he intended to release Jesus. He offered the people a choice. The choice he offered was no doubt aimed at shaming the people into choosing Jesus for release. Thus, he didn't pick a lightweight criminal as the other option; no petty thief, no intoxicated party-goer. He offered Barabbas. Matthew's gospel says that he was a well-known prisoner; Mark's and Luke's gospels say he had committed murder during an insurrection; and John says simply that he had taken part in a rebellion. Insurrection and rebellion against Rome's autonomy was a crime of the highest order. Pilate thought the Jews would be forced to choose Jesus who had not committed any crime over a well-known murderer and insurrectionist. For them to choose Barabbas would be a too blatant demonstration their disloyalty to Caesar, and so they would be forced to choose Jesus. He underestimated their treachery and injustice, and they chose Barabbas anyway. This is where the analogy of the substitute for comparing Isaac and Jesus ends. A substitute was found for Isaac. Jesus did not find a substitute; he was God's substitute, and God's plan of redemption moved ahead as planned.

Barabbas
I digress momentarily from the patriarchs, but I cannot pass over where the analogy breaks down in this story. Why was the side-theme of Barabbas even recorded in the gospel accounts? What does this side-story contribute to our understanding of the death of Jesus?

Barabbas had to know he was facing certain death by crucifixion. We can't help but imagine that he felt like a rabbit in a snake's cage—just biding time, quivering uncontrollably, until a certain hideous death would come upon him. When the officers came to his cell to get him, No doubt he was in utter panic. He thought his time was up. Instead, he was dragged out and released to go free. What did he think just happened? He was soon to learn that Jesus had been condemned in his place.

Pilates's intentions seem obvious. But God had intentions of His own for this encounter with Barabbas. He has another message in this episode for us, looking on. That message is this: Barabbas represents you and me. We are the guilty criminals standing before a holy God. God's reason for Pilate selecting a worst-case criminal was to demonstrate clearly the depth of our own sinful condition. We are sinners, criminals of the highest order, in His holy assessment. In this situation, God demonstrates the extent of our depravity. Then He shows the even greater extent of His grace to us. Now, here we stand in Barabbas' shoes outside the prison of death, and in utter amazement, we behold ourselves set free. Does the perplexed frenzy of Barabbas begin to sink in a little? *By his* [Jesus'] *stripes we are healed. (Isaiah 53:5 NKJ)*

The Analogy
By now, hopefully God's intentional parallelism between Isaac and Jesus should be clear. Isaac is a type of Christ regarding the sacrifice that brings salvation. And yet, you may be wondering, 'Why is this parallelism important? Why do we care?' This significance will be developed in the following discussion.

The most foundational premise for this development is to observe that in this parallelism, if Isaac is a type of Christ, then that suggests Abraham in this narrative is a type of the Heavenly Father. Thus, in relating this story of Abraham, God may be revealing something about Himself.

Abraham's Agony
As already stated, just because this narrative reports the events of this story in a rather matter-of-fact manner is no reason to assume that Abraham was a stoic, unfeeling, man who mechanically obeyed God's command. On the contrary, we can imagine that he suffered every possible torment of the mind and spirit that night, after hearing from God. He was facing having to slay the son he loved so much. Dare to put yourself momentarily in Abrahams's place—it is not a comfortable imagery. It is an unthinkably agonizing one.

In addition to his normal filial emotions, Abraham had even further concerns. Isaac was the embodiment of his hope in the covenant. God Himself had told him it was through Isaac the covenant seed would be sustained. Had God changed His mind? Was God angry at him and perhaps reneging? How could this be? It seemed as if all he had lived for, obeyed, and believed was about to crash and burn. The Hebrews writer in the New Testament refers back to this mental struggle.

Hebrews 11:17-19 (NIV2011)
[17] By faith Abraham, when God tested him, offered Isaac as a sacrifice. He who had embraced the promises was about to sacrifice his one and only son, [18] even though God had said to him, "It is through Isaac that your offspring will be reckoned." [19] Abraham reasoned that God could even raise the dead, and so in a manner of speaking he did receive Isaac back from death.

Abraham likely didn't sleep much that night, or the next three nights. He was in mental and emotional anguish. He tried to rationalize this new command with the promise of Isaac being the promised posterity. He even went so far as to entertain a resurrection from the dead for Isaac. Nevertheless, he obeyed the voice of the Lord.

One other perspective that might tend to moderate this episode for us. We need to eliminate it from doing so in Abraham's story. It is our understanding that God detests child-sacrifice. In our day we might immediately dismiss this command as being inconsistent with our understanding of God. And that is true. Later God would vent wrath toward neighboring nations that practiced child-sacrifice. However, Abraham did not have that in-bred mindset. He himself was taken out of an idolatrous culture. Child sacrifice was likely not as remote from him as it is from us. When he heard God's command, he didn't protest about it being out of character with God. In his mind, there was no nullifying of this command by predisposition.

Our purpose in dwelling on Abraham's emotions does not end with relating. We have a much greater purpose ahead to discover.

God's Passion
We are briefly camping on Abraham's assumed emotions because it seems that they are a picture of God's own passion displayed in the sending of his beloved Son to die for our sins. If it is true that God uses Abraham as a type of Himself in this historical story, then He is intentionally showing us his own agonies, His own pain, His own passion for the souls of lost sinners. When He devised the plan of redemption, it was not simply a legalistic maneuver.

In this story, God is giving us a graphic and intimate look into His own heart, His own turmoil. The type of Christ in Isaac is so obvious, that it is not hard to make that connection. In so doing, it is only the next logical inference to look at Abraham's agony as a type of our heavenly Father's intense pain as a measure of His love for us. In the near-sacrifice of Isaac, He exposes to us a transparency of Himself beyond that displayed anywhere else in scripture. What a poignant and graphic and precious revelation God has shared with us in this Genesis narrative!

> *John 3:16 (NIV2011)*
> *^{16} For God so loved the world that he gave his one and only Son, that whoever believes in him shall not perish but have eternal life.*

God so loved means to convey both quality and quantity of love. Let us not marginalize this precious revelation, or trivialize it by failing to comprehend and ponder its intentional divine disclosure. We must observe this connectedness between Isaac's near-sacrifice and Jesus' sacrifice at Calgary. God wants us to relate to Abraham's anguish during this three-day incident so we can taste of His anguish to the extent humanly possible, to know His heart of love which is so intense that only an intense historical type like this is adequate. He wants us to know the full extent of His passion for our redemption. God spoke from this passion in the great messianic prophecy of Isaiah 53, particularly in this exert.

> *Isaiah 53:10-11 (ESV)*
> *^{10} Yet it was the will of the LORD to crush him; he has put him to grief; when his soul makes an offering for guilt, he shall see his offspring; he shall prolong his days; the will of the LORD shall prosper in his hand. ^{11} Out of the anguish of his soul he shall see and be satisfied; by his knowledge shall the righteous one, my servant, make many to be accounted righteous, and he shall bear their iniquities.*

On this side of the cross, Paul writes to the Romans this short exert packed with the underlying message that the death of Christ was intentional, passionate and sacrificial.

> *Romans 8:32a (ESV)*
> *^{32} He who did not spare his own Son but gave him up for us all . . .*

Imagine you were visiting a good friend who had just lost a loved one in death. What should be your first element of conversation with your friend? Would you begin by discussing who just won the latest ball game or who recently got a new car? Of course you would put everything else aside for a while and share words of comfort with the bereaved friend, expressing shared sorrow, treasured memories and extoling the attributes of the loved one. Any attempt to shift focus from the topic of their sorrow would be insensitive and crude. In the same way, when you realize that in this narrative God has just bared His heart to you, trusting in your empathy, would it not be worse than thoughtless to try to diffuse the dominant subject of thought in your mind just now. If you fail to embrace it, you are like the clumsy, self-centered visitor who avoided the somberness of the bereavement occasion. In this narrative about Abraham and Isaac, God is exposing His own feelings about Jesus' being offered as an atoning sacrifice for our sins. We might say He was 'wearing His emotions on His sleeve' in this episode. Would the holy Creator of the universe and judge of all things stoop to do that? He already has in this historical account.

So intimate is the love God has for us that He desires to share with us heart-to-heart His own passion intensity. So, what should be our response? The degree to which we are able to respond appropriately is conditioned by our perspective of how great God really is. If we wish to bask in His glory in this life, we need to immerse ourselves in the pursuit of knowing His holiness, His greatness, His mercy, His love. Knowing God's intense desire for relationship with us is a step toward appreciating His worth to us.

Together, let us be growing in our knowledge of Him and in our wonder at what He has done and is doing for us. May we be eternally grateful to Jesus who, in obedience to the Father, paid our sin-debt to redeem us from certain destruction.

Chapter 4
The Heart of the Sacrifice

In chapter 3 we looked upon the intense narrative of Abraham being commanded to sacrifice Isaac, his covenant son. We imagined, as much as possible, the emotional agonizing of Abraham through this episode. We drew attention to the obvious and intentional parallel of this near-sacrifice of Isaac with the sacrificial death of Jesus many centuries later. In the context of this parallelism, we identified Isaac and his near-sacrifice as a type of Jesus. We likewise identified Abraham as a type of God the Father during Jesus' torture and crucifixion. This led us to a realization that this whole episode about the near-sacrifice of Isaac was a window into the anguish and passion of God during the crucifixion of Jesus. We tried to grasp the heart of God by viewing the implied turmoil of Abraham.

In this chapter we continue looking at this same Genesis narrative. We wish to view it now through the eyes of Isaac in order to better see the heart of Jesus. This seems appropriate because the scripture portrays Isaac as an ideal type of Christ in the context of this event.

In our Genesis narrative, Isaac is no longer a child. He is a young man, likely in his early to mid-twenties. Abraham is over 110 years old. Isaac could have fought against his father. He could have run away from him. It seems that Isaac could have easily resisted what was happening if he were so inclined to do so.

Yet, he did not resist. Isaac was completely confident in his Father's standing before God. He was also fully invested in the covenant promises and plans of God in which he found himself. Isaac knew full well that he, not his elder half-brother Ishmael, was the covenant offspring of Abraham before God. Isaac was aware that he was God's choice to propagate His plans. That knowledge and that vision made Isaac compliant in this dire situation.

The first and most obvious observation we can make is his willing obedience to Abraham, his father. He stood quietly while Abraham bound him and laid him on the altar of sacrifice. There must have been a moment when it struck him what was happening, but he did not try to escape. Scripture does not record any dialog during this time. Abraham may have begun telling him through sobbing mumbles what the Lord had commanded of him—or maybe not. We don't know. No doubt, Isaac could sense the extreme torment and distress of his father. All we know is Isaac was a compliant sacrifice, an obedient son.

The Passion of Isaac
Just as we said about Abraham in the previous chapter, we can say about Isaac; that although the narrative does not discuss the emotions of Isaac, we cannot presume that Isaac was passive or numbly robotic in his reaction to what was developing. We noted previously that much of Hebrew narrative is written in this factual style, void of commentary about the emotions of those involved. It expected the reader to assume all the appropriate passions and sensations. As faithful readers, we should try to adopt a Jewish mindset for interpreting the narratives. We should assume Isaac experienced normal fears and consternations. We should assume that as this narrative came about, he was in utter anguish. We can know beyond reasonable doubt that two hearts were beating very fast and hard, just then. Yet, he was obedient. He entrusted himself into the hands of his father who he knew loved him dearly.

The Passion of Christ
Likewise, Jesus exercised great passion as he approached the cross, as testifies the writer of Hebrews.

> *Hebrews 12:2 (ESV)*
> *² looking to Jesus, the founder and perfecter of our faith, who for the joy that was set before him endured the cross, despising the shame, and is seated at the right hand of the throne of God.*

That is why the last week of Jesus' incarnation is often called 'passion week.' As the cross loomed close, the passion of Jesus was most evident. It swung from weeping over the imminent fate of Jerusalem to his longing to share his last Passover meal with his disciples. His emotions went from the joy of anticipating awaiting glory, to anguish at Gethsemane anticipating excruciating pain. Note his intensity.

Luke 22:41-44 (ESV)
⁴¹ And he withdrew from them about a stone's throw, and knelt down and prayed, ⁴² saying, "Father, if you are willing, remove this cup from me. Nevertheless, not my will, but yours, be done." ⁴³ And there appeared to him an angel from heaven, strengthening him. ⁴⁴ And being in an agony he prayed more earnestly; and his sweat became like great drops of blood falling down to the ground.

Christ's Obedience to Death on a Cross
In the midst of his agony, Jesus prayed, *Nevertheless, not my will, but yours, be done.* Here we see obedience overruling even the agony of imminent torturous death. This was not a natural reaction to his circumstances. This was his character as God incarnate. It was forecast centuries beforehand as part of the plan in Isaiah's prophetic messianic passage written over 700 years earlier.

Isaiah 53:7 (ESV)
⁷ He was oppressed, and he was afflicted, yet he opened not his mouth; like a lamb that is led to the slaughter, and like a sheep that before its shearers is silent, so he opened not his mouth.

A Matter of Character
Jesus' non-combative character did not just come out during passion week. Once, after healing a crippled man on the sabbath, and knowing the Jewish leaders were plotting to kill him, Jesus withdrew from Jerusalem and went to a more remote place. He might have confronted them and challenged them, but he did not.

Matthew 12:17-21 (ESV)
¹⁷ This was to fulfill what was spoken by the prophet Isaiah: ¹⁸ "Behold, my servant whom I have chosen, my beloved with whom my soul is well pleased. I will put my Spirit upon him, and he will proclaim justice to the Gentiles. ¹⁹ He will not quarrel or cry aloud, nor will anyone hear his voice in the streets; ²⁰ a bruised reed he will not break, and a smoldering wick he will not quench, until he brings justice to victory; ²¹ and in his name the Gentiles will hope."

His gentle attribute characterized his entire earthly ministry. It is not because he did not like confrontation; he had many of those.

He chose to seek obedience to his Father, rather than demand his own rights or preferences. Isaac was like that. He was not only obedient to his father Abraham who was about to sacrifice him on an altar, but later in his life he was also non-combative in relationships. Note this example.

> *Genesis 26:19-22 (NIV2011)*
> [19] *Isaac's servants dug in the valley and discovered a well of fresh water there.* [20] *But the herders of Gerar quarreled with those of Isaac and said, "The water is ours!" So he named the well Esek, because they disputed with him.* [21] *Then they dug another well, but they quarreled over that one also; so he named it Sitnah.* [22] *He moved on from there and dug another well, and no one quarreled over it. He named it Rehoboth, saying, "Now the LORD has given us room and we will flourish in the land."*

Isaac could have demanded his own rights to the well, since his servants had dug it. Instead he called off his herdsmen and chose a peaceful outcome, twice. We might not have made a connection between Isaac and Jesus if it wasn't made obvious for us in the parallelism of the events. But now that it is made clear, we see the similarity of two men who lived in obedience rather than to please themselves.

When Jesus was arrested and taken to Pilate demanding execution, Jesus once again held his peace.

> *John 19:7-11 (ESV)*
> [7] *The Jews answered him, "We have a law, and according to that law he ought to die because he has made himself the Son of God."* [8] *When Pilate heard this statement, he was even more afraid.* [9] *He entered his headquarters again and said to Jesus, "Where are you from?" But Jesus gave him no answer.* [10] *So Pilate said to him, "You will not speak to me? Do you not know that I have authority to release you and authority to crucify you?"* [11] *Jesus answered him, "You would have no authority over me at all unless it had been given you from above. Therefore he who delivered me over to you has the greater sin."*

This non-retaliatory behavior was so significant that Peter testified about it in his first epistle.

1 Peter 2:23-25 (NIV2011)
²³ When they hurled their insults at him, he did not retaliate; when he suffered, he made no threats. Instead, he entrusted himself to him who judges justly. ²⁴ "He himself bore our sins" in his body on the cross, so that we might die to sins and live for righteousness; "by his wounds you have been healed."

The significant prophecy of Isaiah 53 was what the Ethiopian eunuch was reading when the Holy Spirit prompted Phillip to go to the road leading to Gaza from Jerusalem. Phillip heard that catch-phrase being read and used it to introduce the man to the gospel.

Acts 8:29-32 (NKJV)
²⁹ Then the Spirit said to Philip, "Go near and overtake this chariot." ³⁰ So Philip ran to him, and heard him reading the prophet Isaiah, and said, "Do you understand what you are reading?" ³¹ And he said, "How can I, unless someone guides me?" And he asked Philip to come up and sit with him. ³² The place in the Scripture which he read was this: "He was led as a sheep to the slaughter; And as a lamb before its shearer is silent, So He opened not His mouth.

When was Jesus silent? From the time of his arrest, during his hearing before the Sanhedrin, through his trials before Pilot and later Herod, Jesus made no defense plea, no counter accusation, no explanation of his innocence. Before the Sanhedrin, his silence angered the high priest.

Matthew 26:62-63 (ESV)
⁶² And the high priest stood up and said, "Have you no answer to make? What is it that these men testify against you?" ⁶³ But Jesus remained silent. And the high priest said to him, "I adjure you by the living God, tell us if you are the Christ, the Son of God."

We often read of Jesus' sayings while upon the cross in all four of the gospel accounts. In them, we do not find a single insult or curse against those who condemned him or those who carried out the gruesome torture and crucifixion. Jesus did not defend or retaliate because he was being submissive to the will and purpose of his Father. Even though his soul was in anguish, his obedience was unwavering. In this, we see this supreme obedience to his

Father that marked his entire earthly walk. At this point when such dedication became most costly, he remained consistently true to his Father's plan. Thus, his loyalty more greatly shows his passion for what was in front of him and for what lay in the future as a result.

Ultimate Love

Looking back at Abraham and Isaac, may our felt intensity when reading this story mirror for us the passion of both the Father and the Son in the crucifixion of the Son. May we never neglect to cherish the passionate work of both Father and Son in our redemption. Then may we translate that passion into indescribable love. When we fully grasp this level and type of love, all our life should become an act of worship as we seek to honor the Father, Son and Holy Spirit through holy living, motivated by our gratitude and returned love for our God and Savior. May our obedience be motivated by Jesus' and be modeled after him.

1 John 4:19 (NKJV)
[19] We love Him because He first loved us.

Chapter 5
The Dream

What did the patriarchs know? How much did God reveal to them? Abraham, Isaac and Jacob each had their own revelations from God. God spoke to Abraham and Isaac in a way we don't know about. However, we are told how God spoke to Jacob. He spoke to him in a dream; a very special dream.

> *Genesis 28:10-22 (NKJV)*
> *[10] Now Jacob went out from Beersheba and went toward Haran. [11] So he came to a certain place and stayed there all night, because the sun had set. And he took one of the stones of that place and put it at his head, and he lay down in that place to sleep. [12] Then he dreamed, and behold, a ladder was set up on the earth, and its top reached to heaven; and there the angels of God were ascending and descending on it. [13] And behold, the LORD stood above it and said: "I am the LORD God of Abraham your father and the God of Isaac; the land on which you lie I will give to you and your descendants. [14] Also your descendants shall be as the dust of the earth; you shall spread abroad to the west and the east, to the north and the south; and in you and in your seed all the families of the earth shall be blessed. [15] Behold, I am with you and will keep you wherever you go, and will bring you back to this land; for I will not leave you until I have done what I have spoken to you." [16] Then Jacob awoke from his sleep and said, "Surely the LORD is in this place, and I did not know it." [17] And he was afraid and said, "How awesome is this place! This is none other than the house of God, and this is the gate of heaven!" [18] Then Jacob rose early in the morning, and took the stone that he had put at his head, set it up as a pillar, and poured oil on top of it. [19] And he called the name of that place Bethel; but the name of that city had been Luz previously. [20] Then Jacob made a vow, saying, "If God will be with me, and keep me in this way that I am going, and give me bread to eat and clothing to put on, [21] so that I come back to my father's house in peace, then the LORD shall be my God. [22] And this stone*

which I have set as a pillar shall be God's house, and of all that You give me I will surely give a tenth to You."

This dream has been referred to as the vision of 'Jacob's ladder,' Most translations call it a *ladder*, but in some translations it is a staircase. The bottom of the staircase or ladder was resting on the earth, while the top reached into heaven. The stairs provided direct angelic interaction between heaven and earth. It was a well-traveled staircase, as multiple angels ascended and descended. Most prominently, there above it stood the *LORD*. The Lord spoke to Jacob, giving to him essentially a repeat of the covenant promises that He had given Abraham, and later, Isaac.

Awakening

At this point in his life, Jacob was well aware of the covenant promises made by God to Abraham and to Isaac. He had been taught them by his father Isaac. He was more than aware of them--he treasured them in his heart and sought in his own selfish ambition to acquire them. This point should not be overlooked. For all of his faults, the one redeeming virtue of Jacob was that he cherished the God-given birthright of his father and grandfather. That was no small thing. It is pointed out in scripture that, in contrast, his brother Esau despised his birthright.

> *Hebrews 12:16-17 (NIV2011)*
> *[16] See that no one is sexually immoral, or is godless like Esau, who for a single meal sold his inheritance rights as the oldest son. [17] Afterward, as you know, when he wanted to inherit this blessing, he was rejected. Even though he sought the blessing with tears, he could not change what he had done.*

Jacob valued the birthright and the patriarchal blessing, and that was foundational to the faith God was creating within him. Nevertheless, prior to this point, they were inherited promises. His faith was an inherited faith. For Jacob, at this point it was an inheritance of offspring and land.

So it can be with us. If we have always grown up in a family of faith and a congregation of believers, we are blessed indeed. However, there comes a point in every person's life when he or she must personally embrace God on His terms. You cannot inherit faith. You can learn faith, but you cannot get it through inheritance. One must take responsibility to respond to God's upward call. Usually it is a process. Sometimes it is all-at-once. The end result is the evidence.

In Jacob's case, it was a process that led to dependent faith. This dream was not what immediately changed his character, but it was the beginning of a series of events. Ultimately he was able to bless his twelve sons and to prophetically tell the role each would fill. Near the end of his life, when he and his whole family moved to Egypt to escape the famine in the promised land, Jacob met face-to-face for the first time with the pharaoh of Egypt, the most powerful man on earth. When asked about himself, Jacob described his life like this:

> *Genesis 47:7-10 (NKJV)*
> *⁷ Then Joseph brought in his father Jacob and set him before Pharaoh; and Jacob blessed Pharaoh. ⁸ Pharaoh said to Jacob, "How old are you?" ⁹ And Jacob said to Pharaoh, "The days of the years of my pilgrimage are one hundred and thirty years; few and evil have been the days of the years of my life, and they have not attained to the days of the years of the life of my fathers in the days of their pilgrimage." ¹⁰ So Jacob blessed Pharaoh, and went out from before Pharaoh.*

When he stood before pharaoh, Jacob knew his greatest obstacle had been himself, his ambitious greed, his selfish and deceitful ways, his independent spirit. But this proclamation to pharaoh occurred much later than the time of the dream. It had followed a long process. He then had a much clearer vision of his birthright under the covenant.

Our current narrative about Jacob's dream was the beginning of that process, at a time when the vision was not so clear to him. In this dream, God's covenant with Jacob was personally confirmed. In this dream, God showed Jacob that the promises made to Abraham and to Isaac were still promised to him. Jacob had a long way to go, but this was an awakening of Jacob to begin to trust in his God.

The Surpassing Significance of the Dream

The dream confirmed the divine covenant, which was very important in God's plan to accomplish His redemptive purpose. The most obvious elements of God's promises were numerous children and grandchildren, land, and a means through which God would bless mankind through him. Offspring and homeland could be envisioned. The promise to bless all nations through Jacob—not so much. How did Jacob perceive that aspect of the covenant? What was meant by the flow of angelic beings up and down the ladder? What message did he understand from this dream?

Most obviously, the ascending and descending of angels demonstrated that God was involved with Jacob's affairs on earth. It shows God dispatching angels to and from actual earthly situations, orchestrating things to suit His purposes. God's involvement is not always evident in the moment. Jacob said, *surely the Lord is in this place, and I did not know it*. We may feel like victims of circumstance. Here we see God exercising his oversight, and his sovereignty. How extensive is His oversight? We cannot know this from this passage. One thing we can learn is that God is available, and that He exercises His sovereignty in each situation to the extent that He wishes.

Furthermore, we see in this the promise of protection. Jacob is fleeing for his life. He knows he is taking a temporary sojourn to escape the wrath of his brother Esau, but that he will eventually face him again. God will not leave him to fend for himself, but will go with him. Since it is God's stated intention to bring Jacob back here to Canaan and give to him the land, the descendants, and so forth, it is incumbent on God to keep him from being killed prematurely. This concept is intrinsic to the vision message.

Likewise, we see God's promise to keep us as New Testament believers. Of course we don't know how that translates in His purposeful scheme in terms of length of life, or in prosperity, or in temporal happiness. We simply find peace in knowing that God is walking with us to keep us for His ultimate purpose, and our own ultimate blessing.

There may be another message given to Jacob in this dream, though a veiled message, so that perhaps it was not for him to understand, but was actually a message given to him, but for us. This other message has to do with the ladder itself, seeing it as emblematic. Perhaps you have seen the Campus Crusade evangelistic tract using the analogy of a deep and wide chasm, and on one side of the chasm is you. On the other side is God. This demonstrates the separation of men from God caused by sin. It is a separation that leaves you helpless and hopeless based on your own abilities to overcome it. Then the analogy introduces a footbridge across that chasm, allowing you to cross over to God. That footbridge is identified as Jesus. He is the way to God. If we take Campus Crusade's horizontal separation model and rotate it ninety degrees so that God's side of the chasm is on top and our side is on bottom, we have the picture revealed in this dream. This dream presents a vertical view of this separation chasm model. It shows a way of connectedness to God in the ladder. Can it be that Jesus was in view in this ancient prophecy? Can it be that he is the ladder or staircase into heaven? We might consider this analogy a stretch, if not for the fact that Jesus made this statement about himself.

> *John 1:49-51 (NIV2011)*
> *[49] Then Nathanael declared, "Rabbi, you are the Son of God; you are the king of Israel." [50] Jesus said, "You believe because I told you I saw you under the fig tree. You will see greater things than that." [51] He then added, "Very truly I tell you, you will see 'heaven open, and the angels of God ascending and descending on' the Son of Man."*

In this passage, Jesus seems to draw from the language and imagery of Jacob's ladder. He seems to be connecting the dots for us that he is, in fact, the ladder in Jacob's dream. Notice that there are no other ladders, no other means of connection between heaven and earth in this dream. This is consistent with what Jesus told his disciples.

> *John 14:5-6 (NIV2011)*
> *[5] Thomas said to him, "Lord, we don't know where you are going, so how can we know the way?" [6] Jesus answered, "I am the way and the truth and the life. No one comes to the Father except through me.*

No one comes to the Father except through Jesus. No one. A whole chapter could be written on verse six of this passage, but let us summarize it in context. We can always tell the mindset of the reader when we hear it quoted verbally. Most often it is read in a monotone voice. *I am the way and the truth and the life.* In this rendition, the emphasis is on the three objects: way, truth, and life. This could spawn a whole study in itself, and what a study it would be. Another rendition that is occasionally heard emphasizes the words ***I am***. This emphasis sees Jesus as the great *I AM* of Exodus, and links it with many other New Testament *I am* statements. The theological assertion of this emphasis is that Jesus is God, the God of the Old Testament, the God of Abraham, and of Isaac, and of Jacob. What a great study that is. But as great as those themes are, I think the central idea, in context, is conveyed by emphasizing only the word *I*. Thomas has just told Jesus he doesn't know the way, and Jesus says, *I* (emphasis) *am the way.* Not a direction. Not a literal footpath to be followed. Not an event. Not a religion. He personally is the only way to God. In other words, to render its meaning this way, we understand Jesus as saying, 'I, myself, am the way.' And this rendition is emphasized by the words that follow, *No one comes to the Father except through me.*

One day, Peter stood before the Jewish rulers, defending his reason for preaching Jesus. He repeated the one-way-only message that Jesus had proclaimed. He boldly told them:

Acts 4:12 (NIV2011)
[12] Salvation is found in no one else, for there is no other name under heaven given to mankind by which we must be saved."

It appears the one path to God in Jacob's dream is Jesus, symbolized by the ladder. Of course we cannot say how much of this analogy was understood by Jacob. One thing we can know. God speaks to us through those Old Testament situations. We are able to see Jesus as the bridge to heaven, the only bridge. Thus, it is not as important to know precisely the extent of Jacob's understanding as it is to realize that He is speaking to us. We are reminded of this throughout both the Old and New Testaments:

Psalm 102:18 (NIV2011)
[18] Let this be written for a future generation, that a people not yet created may praise the LORD:

Romans 4:23-24 (NIV2011)
[23] The words "it was credited to him" were written not for him alone, [24] but also for us, to whom God will credit righteousness—for us who believe in him who raised Jesus our Lord from the dead.

Chapter 6
The Wrestler

Job 33:14 (NIV2011)
¹⁴ For God does speak—now one way, now another—though no one perceives it.

Hebrews 1:1 (NIV2011)
¹ In the past God spoke to our ancestors through the prophets at many times and in various ways,

One of the strangest ways God has ever spoken took place in the life of Jacob. Jacob was a twin with his brother Esau. In the womb the twins *struggled* with each other. It is noted in scripture that Esau was born first, but that Jacob grasped his brother's heel as he was birthed. This grasping signified the tenor of their early lives during which Jacob seized the birthright from his brother by bribery, and his father's blessing by deception. Jacob's covetous aspirations are described beginning in Genesis 25:19 and continuing through Genesis 33. I recommend you read it if you are not familiar with the story, but because of its longevity, we won't present it here.

Jacob's Situation
Their relationship can be summarized by noting that Esau was a man who lived for the moment's pleasure, while depreciating his role as Isaac's firstborn son and potential heir to God's covenant. His appetites were mostly sensual. On the other hand, Jacob had his sights set on obtaining those privileges and did so with intentional resolve, but used unscrupulous means. His appetites were more visionary, albeit self-serving. As a result, Jacob stole the blessing of his father through deceit and infuriated Esau to the point that Esau wanted to kill his brother.

Jacob fled the land, returning to Abraham's original homeland, and to his mother Rebecca's brother, Laban. While living there, he married Laban's two daughters and their two handmaids, had children, and was exceedingly fruitful and prosperous. For fourteen years, Jacob indentured himself to Laban, his father-in-law. Finally, the Lord spoke to Jacob and told him to return to the covenant land. And so he did. That leaving was an adventure in itself, but in summary, Jacob was adversarial with his father-in-law Laban and in danger from him. God worked in the situation to soften Laban's heart and bring about reconciliation.

Jacob's Faith a Work in Progress

Through all this, Jacob was a man of questionable ethics and shaded motive. While he earnestly valued the birthright of the covenant, he did not hesitate to use deceit to attain it or to attain anything else he wanted. His loyalties were to himself. He had received blessings from God and promises from God. He had even received a message in a dream of God's providence over him. Yet in his character, he remained a rascal, living by carnal predisposition rather than by true faith. So thus, the stage is set for our focal narrative of this chapter.

Jacob obeyed the instruction of the Lord to return to Canaan. As he did so, he knew he must encounter his twin brother, Esau. He had had no contact with Esau since leaving Canaan, but he had known when he left that Esau planned to kill him. This loomed large in his path to obedience, and he was terrified to meet Esau.

Genesis 32:3-16 (NKJV)
³ Then Jacob sent messengers before him to Esau his brother in the land of Seir, the country of Edom. ⁴ And he commanded them, saying, "Speak thus to my lord Esau, 'Thus your servant Jacob says: "I have dwelt with Laban and stayed there until now. ⁵ I have oxen, donkeys, flocks, and male and female servants; and I have sent to tell my lord, that I may find favor in your sight." ' " ⁶ Then the messengers returned to Jacob, saying, "We came to your brother Esau, and he also is coming to meet you, and four hundred men are with him." ⁷ So Jacob was greatly afraid and distressed; and he divided the people that were with him, and the flocks and herds and camels, into two companies. ⁸ And he said, "If Esau comes to the one company and attacks it, then the other company which is left will escape." ⁹ Then Jacob said, "O God of my father Abraham and God of my father Isaac, the LORD who said to me, 'Return to your country and to your family, and I will deal well with you': ¹⁰ I am not worthy of the least of all the mercies and of all the truth which You have shown Your servant; for I crossed over this Jordan with my staff, and now I have become two companies. ¹¹ Deliver me, I pray, from the hand of my brother, from the hand of Esau; for I fear him, lest he come and attack me and the mother with

the children. ¹² For You said, 'I will surely treat you well, and make your descendants as the sand of the sea, which cannot be numbered for multitude.' " ¹³ So he lodged there that same night, and took what came to his hand as a present for Esau his brother: ¹⁴ two hundred female goats and twenty male goats, two hundred ewes and twenty rams, ¹⁵ thirty milk camels with their colts, forty cows and ten bulls, twenty female donkeys and ten foals. ¹⁶ Then he delivered them to the hand of his servants, every drove by itself, and said to his servants, "Pass over before me, and put some distance between successive droves."

His attempt at procuring reconciliation consisted of sending gifts from his own wealth. With Esau coming to meet him with a formidable fighting force, Jacob turns to God. He prepares as best as he is able, hoping for an amiable reception, but he realizes his only hope lies with God. While he had previously lived in the promises of God, this may have been the first time he could not take matters into his own hands, and the first time he realized his total dependence on God. He was at the end of his rope. Jacob was desperate. This desperation set up the strange encounter that is the theme for this chapter.

Genesis 32:22-31 (NKJV)
²² And he arose that night and took his two wives, his two female servants, and his eleven sons, and crossed over the ford of Jabbok. ²³ He took them, sent them over the brook, and sent over what he had. ²⁴ Then Jacob was left alone; and a Man wrestled with him until the breaking of day. ²⁵ Now when He saw that He did not prevail against him, He touched the socket of his hip; and the socket of Jacob's hip was out of joint as He wrestled with him. ²⁶ And He said, "Let Me go, for the day breaks." But he said, "I will not let You go unless You bless me!" ²⁷ So He said to him, "What is your name?" He said, "Jacob." ²⁸ And He said, "Your name shall no longer be called Jacob, but Israel; for you have struggled with God and with men, and have prevailed." ²⁹ Then Jacob asked, saying, "Tell me Your name, I pray." And He said, "Why is it that you ask about My name?" And He blessed him there. ³⁰ And Jacob called the name of the place Peniel: "For I have seen God face to face, and my life is preserved." ³¹ Just as he crossed over Penuel the sun rose on him, and he limped on his hip.

This story ends with God intervening and softening Esau's heart, making for an amicable reunion. In this way, Jacob's life was spared from the wrath of Esau.

Wrestling With a Friend

Perhaps the obvious first question about this mysterious encounter is, 'Who is this person with whom Jacob wrestled?' In verse 30 of the narrative, Jacob says he saw God face-to-face. Much later near the end of his life Jacob would bless his sons, saying:

> *Genesis 48:16 (NIV2011)*
> *[16] the Angel who has delivered me from all harm —may he bless these boys. May they be called by my name and the names of my fathers Abraham and Isaac, and may they increase greatly on the earth."*

Here he identifies that an angel changed the mind of his brother Esau, inferring him to be the same person with whom he wrestled at Bethel. Who was this man with whom he wrestled? What does it have to do with us? Whatever else we learn, it is clear that something significant happened there. Jacob perceived that he saw God face-to-face. Much later, the prophet spoke of him, saying:

> *Hosea 12:2-5 (NIV2011)*
> *[2] The LORD has a charge to bring against Judah; he will punish Jacob according to his ways and repay him according to his deeds. [3] In the womb he grasped his brother's heel; as a man he struggled with God. [4] He struggled with the angel and overcame him; he wept and begged for his favor. He found him at Bethel and talked with him there— [5] the LORD God Almighty, the LORD is his name!*

Hosea said that Jacob struggled with God. In context, the prophet is accusing the nations of Israel and Judah of their waywardness. He is momentarily looking backward, not forward, showing how they were wayward from their very inception in the life of their father Jacob. As Jacob was rebellious, so followed this stiff-necked people.

In our main text of Genesis 38, the One who wrestled with Jacob is referred to as a 'man,' while Jacob believed he saw God face-to-face. In Genesis 48 Jacob himself calls him an 'Angel.' Hosea, speaking by the power of the Holy Spirit, tells more detail than in Genesis and calls him both 'the Angel' and 'God.' Some Jewish scholars believe this was a theophany—God in human form. Many Christians believe this was a 'christophany,' that is, a bodily appearance of Christ occurring prior to his incarnation in Bethlehem, occurring during the Old Testament time period. This passage is one of several Old Testament references to a pre-incarnate appearance of Christ under the description of 'The Angel of the Lord.' Both Jacob and the prophet said it was God with whom he wrestled, and Hosea clarifies further that it was *the LORD God Almighty, the LORD is his name!*

Thus, for some extended time, Jacob had a literal, physical wrestling match with God (feasibly Christ) who came to him in bodily form. And Jacob discerned that this was a divine encounter. Jacob was not simply having a talk with God. He was contending with God. He was pushing and pulling against God. While he was trying to not be overpowered by God, he was also holding his own with God, as God allowed.

Why Did Jacob Wrestle?

The Genesis narrative tells us precious little about this wrestling match. It only mentions the physical aspect of the struggle except when Jacob asks for the blessing of his contender. The greater textual space is given to that conversation. What was the essence of this struggle? It appears that Jacob was not afraid of the man with whom he wrestled, as he might have been if fighting an enemy. What significant thing was happening?

Most certainly, what was at stake in this struggle was the issue of sovereignty and lordship. In the past, Jacob had been his own lord. Oh, he had formally acknowledged God as sovereign, but the way he had conducted his life testified of a self-serving heart. Jacob's problem was that he was not leading a life surrendered to God's will. He was living life like an unbeliever, like a non-covenant, worldly person. He was doing exactly what he desired rather than what God wanted for him.

In this wrestling struggle, we see Jacob's self-will and God's purposes thrown into an arena together. One must eventually give in to the other. It was a strange dynamic. Jacob eagerly contends with God, believing that it is indeed God with whom he is wrestling. He is seeking God's blessing, while simultaneously trying to impose his own will. It was a long and difficult struggle for Jacob, lasting from some time in the middle of the night until dawn. It was long and difficult because self-will is such an entrenched part of mortal man that it is not easy to let go. It is a big difference that can separate a verbal commitment--a commitment in principle, and a truly surrendered life. It can only happen under the power of God's Holy Spirit which brings regeneration and renewal.

While Jacob is said to have prevailed, what does that mean? It does not mean Jacob won and got his way. Rather it means that Jacob prevailed by clinging to the One who had the blessing he sought. He refused to let go of the man, God in flesh, without knowing he was in His will. God then blessed Jacob by promising him regeneration through a new name. His birth name Jacob which meant "supplanter" was changed to *Israel; for you have struggled with God and with men, and have prevailed.* This was the beginning of genuine devotion to God as Sovereign Lord in Jacob's life.

The Word Applied
While we understand this narrative as a real, historical event in the life of Jacob, it most certainly was a spiritual benchmark in his life. Likewise, the principle has application for us. When we seek God earnestly in prayer, sometimes the first order of business is one of lordship. Do we approach God with requests that benefit us and our own wishes? We may need to wrestle with the lordship issue before He can bless us with His purposes.

It is teaching us something about God. It is teaching us something about how we interact with God; how we pray. No other passage more graphically portrays this. Therefore, we will consider this application to our own prayers.

What does wrestling in prayer look like? If you have earnestly prayed before, seeking a specific answer, then it is likely you have struggled in prayer already.

Perhaps early in your life of faith, when a prayer wasn't answered in the manner you wished, did it not create a bit of a faith crisis, a rather consternating and disturbing time? When this happened, and happened again, how did you pray the next time? Did you not quickly learn that to avoid these faith crises, you should pray safer prayers? You learned to pray in a way that left God plenty of wiggle room. In the process, you inadvertently learned to not trust

God with the important issues of life. Yet, gradually your faith began to grow back, and you once again dared to pray in faith. At just the right time, God sent an answer to confirm your trust. You have wrestled with God, and have prevailed. You clung to Him even when not understanding His plans, not seeing His response.

Or perhaps you have prayed for something you considered significant without receiving an answer. You persisted in prayer over a long time. Whether or not you got the answer you were seeking, you wrestled with God. You prevailed in that you continued to pray with faith, in spite of no immediate confirming evidence. Perhaps you have had a crisis situation, and out of desperation, you prayed with passionate intensity. You pleaded, begged, reasoned, even challenged God's character. You wrestled with God. These are some of the behaviors we exhibit when wrestling with God.

At this point, maybe you are wondering if perhaps I am exercising too much conjecture by taking an obscure story and trying to make it more representative than it is intended to be. Maybe you think I am presuming too much; spiritualizing something that wasn't intended to be spiritualized. If so, then please consider just a few out of many examples of this type of praying, given in scripture.

Biblical Examples of Wrestling in Prayer
The Bible is filled with examples where the person praying had to struggle or contend with God or with Jesus. Here are a few of the more obvious ones, starting in the Old Testament, and moving into the New Testament. This is just a brief sampling, not a comprehensive collection.

> *Genesis 18:22-33 (NKJV)*
> *[22] Then the men turned away from there and went toward Sodom, but Abraham still stood before the LORD. [23] And Abraham came near and said, "Would You also destroy the righteous with the wicked? [24] Suppose there were fifty righteous within the city; would You also destroy the place and not spare it for the fifty righteous that were in it? [25] Far be it from You to do such a thing as this, to slay the righteous with the wicked, so that the righteous should be as the wicked; far be it from You! Shall not the Judge of all the earth do right?" [26] So the LORD said, "If I find in Sodom fifty righteous within the city, then I will spare all the place for their sakes." [27] Then Abraham answered and said,*

"Indeed now, I who am but dust and ashes have taken it upon myself to speak to the Lord: ^{28} *Suppose there were five less than the fifty righteous; would You destroy all of the city for lack of five?" So He said, "If I find there forty-five, I will not destroy it."* ^{29} *And he spoke to Him yet again and said, "Suppose there should be forty found there?" So He said, "I will not do it for the sake of forty."* ^{30} *Then he said, "Let not the Lord be angry, and I will speak: Suppose thirty should be found there?" So He said, "I will not do it if I find thirty there."* ^{31} *And he said, "Indeed now, I have taken it upon myself to speak to the Lord: Suppose twenty should be found there?" So He said, "I will not destroy it for the sake of twenty."* ^{32} *Then he said, "Let not the Lord be angry, and I will speak but once more: Suppose ten should be found there?" And He said, "I will not destroy it for the sake of ten."* ^{33} *So the LORD went His way as soon as He had finished speaking with Abraham; and Abraham returned to his place.*

Wow! It reads as if Abraham stepped in front of the Lord and blocked his way of passage, while the two other messengers went on ahead. In verse 25, if I had never read this before, I might anticipate that verse 26 would read, "Then God struck Abraham down and he died." But no! God was intentionally drawing Abraham into a dialog of contention. Later, not once, but twice, God baited Moses to contend for the Israelites.

Exodus 32:9-14 (ESV)
^{9} *And the LORD said to Moses, "I have seen this people, and behold, it is a stiff-necked people.* ^{10} *Now therefore let me alone, that my wrath may burn hot against them and I may consume them, in order that I may make a great nation of you."* ^{11} *But Moses implored the LORD his God and said, "O LORD, why does your wrath burn hot against your people, whom you have brought out of the land of Egypt with great power and with a mighty hand?* ^{12} *Why should the Egyptians say, 'With evil intent did he bring them out, to kill them in the mountains and to consume them from the face of the earth'? Turn from your burning anger and relent from this disaster against your people.* ^{13} *Remember Abraham, Isaac, and Israel, your servants, to whom you swore by your own self, and said to them, 'I will multiply your offspring as the stars of heaven, and all this land that I have promised I will give to your offspring, and they shall*

inherit it forever.'" ¹⁴ And the LORD relented from the disaster that he had spoken of bringing on his people.

Numbers 14:11-20 (ESV)
¹¹ And the LORD said to Moses, "How long will this people despise me? And how long will they not believe in me, in spite of all the signs that I have done among them? ¹² I will strike them with the pestilence and disinherit them, and I will make of you a nation greater and mightier than they." ¹³ But Moses said to the LORD, "Then the Egyptians will hear of it, for you brought up this people in your might from among them, ¹⁴ and they will tell the inhabitants of this land. They have heard that you, O LORD, are in the midst of this people. For you, O LORD, are seen face to face, and your cloud stands over them and you go before them, in a pillar of cloud by day and in a pillar of fire by night. ¹⁵ Now if you kill this people as one man, then the nations who have heard your fame will say, ¹⁶ 'It is because the LORD was not able to bring this people into the land that he swore to give to them that he has killed them in the wilderness.' ¹⁷ And now, please let the power of the Lord be great as you have promised, saying, ¹⁸ 'The LORD is slow to anger and abounding in steadfast love, forgiving iniquity and transgression, but he will by no means clear the guilty, visiting the iniquity of the fathers on the children, to the third and the fourth generation.' ¹⁹ Please pardon the iniquity of this people, according to the greatness of your steadfast love, just as you have forgiven this people, from Egypt until now." ²⁰ Then the LORD said, "I have pardoned, according to your word.

Much later, God was about to bring judgment on Israel for their lawlessness and injustice. He pronounced his charges against them, and said this.

Ezekiel 22:30-31 (NIV2011)
³⁰ "I looked for someone among them who would build up the wall and stand before me in the gap on behalf of the land so I would not have to destroy it, but I found no one. ³¹ So I will pour out my wrath on them and consume them with my fiery anger, bringing down on their own heads all they have done, declares the Sovereign LORD."

God was seeking someone to contend with Him over the cause of Israel, but he found no one. The imagery of building up the walls and standing in the gap was forward-looking to what would occur about 148 years later during the time of Nehemiah. Nehemiah would oversee the rebuilding of the walls of Jerusalem while under danger from outside attack. Guards were posted in all the breeches until repairs were finished. In this Ezekiel passage, the imagery is not only forward-looking to the days of Nehemiah, but is also symbolic. God is the outside threat, and He seeks an advocate for the people who would defend against Himself on their behalf. Because he did not find anyone who would contend with Him, he destroyed the land. God looked for an advocate, one who would wrestle with Him, yet without finding one. Now that destruction was not terminal for the nation, and it led eventually to the Nehemiah episode.

We have been given a marvelous opportunity and responsibility in the gift of prayer. We are made responsible to intercede for one another. We are called to enter into prayer with such a sense of its power and privilege that we do it with passionate resolve. The resolve he wants from us is not passive acquiescence, but an expectant zeal for the cause of those for whom we are praying. When we see circumstances not lining up for blessing, we contend with God over the matter.

In the New Testament, there are many examples of struggling with the Lord. In them, it is clear that Jesus is intentionally creating that struggle.

> *Matthew 15:21-28 (NKJV)*
> *[21] Then Jesus went out from there and departed to the region of Tyre and Sidon. [22] And behold, a woman of Canaan came from that region and cried out to Him, saying, "Have mercy on me, O Lord, Son of David! My daughter is severely demon-possessed." [23] But He answered her not a word. And His disciples came and urged Him, saying, "Send her away, for she cries out after us." [24] But He answered and said, "I was not sent except to the lost sheep of the house of Israel." [25] Then she came and worshiped Him, saying, "Lord, help me!" [26] But He answered and said, "It is not good to take the children's bread and throw it to the little dogs." [27] And she said, "Yes, Lord, yet even the little dogs eat the crumbs which fall from their masters' table." [28] Then Jesus answered and said to her, "O woman, great is your*

faith! Let it be to you as you desire." And her daughter was healed from that very hour.

A casual reading of this might make us think that Jesus was rather rude to the woman. But in light of our observation of 'struggling' in prayer being so common, we see that Jesus was truly caring about her from the beginning. But first, she had to contend with Jesus a bit to demonstrate her faith for herself as well as the disciples to see. She grew in faith through both the wrestling and the healing. On another occasion Jesus told this parable.

> *Luke 11:5-8 (NIV2011)*
> *⁵ Then Jesus said to them, "Suppose you have a friend, and you go to him at midnight and say, 'Friend, lend me three loaves of bread; ⁶ a friend of mine on a journey has come to me, and I have no food to offer him.' ⁷ And suppose the one inside answers, 'Don't bother me. The door is already locked, and my children and I are in bed. I can't get up and give you anything.' ⁸ I tell you, even though he will not get up and give you the bread because of friendship, yet because of your shameless audacity he will surely get up and give you as much as you need.*

Because of the neighbor's *shameless audacity*, that is his boldness coupled with persistence, his request was met. God is teaching us to intercede for others with such tenacity that it becomes a wrestling match with God. Friend who was aroused from sleep by his neighbor represents God by contrast. The contrast is that the friend was reluctant while God is eager to bless us.

Jesus demonstrated this wrestling in prayer in his own life. He had no greater intensity in prayer than that in Gethsemane. The agony of anticipation over what lay ahead challenged his obedience to the Father like nothing else had. No other human could have faced such a horrific destiny with such confident faith.

> *Luke 22:44 (NIV2011)*
> *⁴⁴ And being in anguish, he prayed more earnestly, and his sweat was like drops of blood falling to the ground.*

> *Hebrews 5:7 (NIV2011)*
> *⁷ During the days of Jesus' life on earth, he offered up prayers and petitions with fervent cries and tears to the one*

who could save him from death, and he was heard because of his reverent submission.

God did not save him from death. He saved him from permanent death by raising him. Thus, we see God's solution to our issues is not always that of our choosing, but often reflects God's bigger purposes.

Such wrestling in prayer is a holy moment before God. He cherishes it as the praying one earnestly seeks for Him, having his faith stretched. Paul speaks to us of his own struggle with God over his *thorn in the flesh*. The end result was a whole new perspective of God's power in the face of his own weakness.

> *2 Corinthians 12:7-10 (NKJV)*
> *[7] And lest I should be exalted above measure by the abundance of the revelations, a thorn in the flesh was given to me, a messenger of Satan to buffet me, lest I be exalted above measure. [8] Concerning this thing I pleaded with the Lord three times that it might depart from me. [9] And He said to me, "My grace is sufficient for you, for My strength is made perfect in weakness." Therefore most gladly I will rather boast in my infirmities, that the power of Christ may rest upon me. [10] Therefore I take pleasure in infirmities, in reproaches, in needs, in persecutions, in distresses, for Christ's sake. For when I am weak, then I am strong.*

Do You Ever Wrestle?

When we communicate with God, we call it prayer. Not all prayers are contending prayers. Struggling with God may not be the most common approach in prayer. Prayer should most often be a joyful experience. But is there a danger that our prayers can become too casual? We should be confident in entering before God, but not casual and comfortable. Struggling in prayer helps us define and measure the essence of our faith. In fact, prayer is conversation with an all-powerful God with whom we have a loving relationship. Our regular praying should spring from the joy of that relationship. When we offer praise and thanksgiving, it should come from a glad heart. In it, God gives you expression of your love for Him.

However, when you need to get serious with God, whether from desperation, or from desired deeper devotion, or for whatever reason, you can expect Him to test your tenacity. Jacob struggled in prayer that night as he wrestled in a way that exceeded mere conversation. It was a real, physical encounter. So too with us. We should be prepared for a time of contention to test and shape our priorities and loyalties. In those prayers, God is not asking, "How much do you love Me?', but rather 'How much do you trust Me?' In that case, will you refuse to let Him go until He blesses you?

Desperate Jacob needed God's blessing of protection. He refused to let go of the messenger until he had an answer from him. He clung to him in his desperation, knowing that God was his one and only hope, his one and only salvation from the trouble ahead. The messenger purposely reined in his full power so that Jacob could prevail. He intended for Jacob to prevail, but only after a struggle. For emphasis, I say again that the messenger intended for Jacob to prevail, but not without a struggle; a faith-changing struggle. In this, we discover a principle of God's dealing with human nature. It is not necessarily an absolute principle, but one that God employs from time to time when he knows it is needed. It is this. God does not always give us a quick and easy answer to our prayer requests. Sometimes he draws us out so as to deepen our dependency on Him. Jesus taught his disciples this principle.

Luke 18:1 (NIV2011)
¹ Then Jesus told his disciples a parable to show them that they should always pray and not give up.

His parable was that of the unjust judge and the widow. He was teaching them to become wrestlers with God, just like the widow 'wrestled' with the judge. Paul set examples of both himself and Epaphras as intercessors for the believers of Colossae to emulate.

Colossians 2:1 (NIV2011)
¹ I want you to know how hard I am contending for you and for those at Laodicea, and for all who have not met me personally.

Colossians 4:12 (NIV2011)
¹² Epaphras, who is one of you and a servant of Christ Jesus, sends greetings. He is always wrestling in prayer for you, that you may stand firm in all the will of God, mature and fully assured.

In this Colossians passage, *he is always wrestling in prayer for you,* this may be a metaphorical reference to our story of Jacob's wrestling match. The situation for which Epaphras was praying wasn't a crisis situation. It was his routine way of praying for them. The struggle for Epaphras was not because of desperation. Rather it was from a cogent assessment of the elevated priority of their faith, for which he was praying.

Expect to Wrestle
God often extends our faith by making us wrestle in prayer. He expects it. He often requires it. It is so common in scripture that we need to take careful note of its appropriateness in our own prayers.

One practical way we can enter this type of praying is through fasting. Fasting is not commanded in the New Testament, but it is assumed. Jesus said, *When you fast . . .* Fasting is the abstinence from food for the purpose of enhancing one's relationship and audience with God. Unfortunately, fasting among believers is not so commonly practiced in our culture of material affluence and personal independence. Those who do fast, soon realize that it is a way to struggle, to wrestle, to contend with God that takes heartfelt praying to a higher level. In the first chapter we discussed living as pilgrims in this world. Fasting is the exercise of that concept in the realm of prayer. In fasting, we learn to elevate eternal priorities in prayer over temporal priorities. Fasting and prayer together is a wrestling match between our flesh and God's purposes. When you do it, expect your priorities to be rearranged. Expect God to answer in an unexpected manner. Expect that God just might show Himself.

Do you frequently wrestle in prayer? If not, why not? God not only allows you to do so, but He intends for you to do so. It is part of a process that only God fully understands. Just as we don't have to know the technology behind a microwave in order to use one, likewise, we don't have to fully understand the mind of God to be obedient to his instructions to us. From scripture, we realize that we are called to wrestle with Him in prayer over life's issues.

One more comment on our text is in order. Notice that in the whole episode, Jacob never feared the man with whom he wrestled. Such wrestling is not an unpleasant experience. It should not be approached with apprehension. On the contrary, it is for the joy set before you that you seek to enter into such a contest. It is an intriguing arena of your will mingled with God's goals. Just as Jacob did not fear the nighttime wrestler, so we should not be intimidated by wrestling with a God who loves us so much that He gave His only begotten Son to redeem us. Embrace this wrestling match with enthusiasm and boldness, refusing to not be heard. Even in the face of desperate necessity, eagerly enter into this union as into the ultimate answer-source for your need. However, don't wrestle with the idea of imposing your will over God's, but rather to expose your will in earnestness and resolve, trusting in His outcome. Just as Jacob was said to have *overcome* in his match with God, he did not defeat God's purpose. God had His way with Jacob. God changed his name from Jacob (supplanter) to Israel (overcomer), and it was at this point that He began to rearrange Jacob's priorities.

We often hear about being a prayer warrior. We are called to that. In that venue, we are struggling against a true adversary, the devil, who desires to destroy us, and we are told to utilize the spiritual armor God provides to defeat him and to protect ourselves. However, in this wrestling of which we are speaking, our wrestling partner is God, and we wrestle or contend at His bidding. This wrestling may feel somewhat adversarial, but we are wrestling with a friend, not an enemy. Wrestle with a resolve born of love for God and others. If not, wrestle with a desire to obtain that kind of love. God seeks this kind of relationship with you and me. Become a prayer wrestler as well as a prayer warrior.

Chapter 7
The Patriarchs Still Speak

It might be easy for us to dismiss these early Old Testament narratives as ancient history. After all, we now have the whole remaining Old Testament and the New Testament behind us to give us a more current update of God's dealings with us. What could we learn from these old stories?

Perhaps the best response to that question is to point out the vast number of times both Old and New Testaments make reference back to these ancient narratives, often quoting from them. There are timeless, foundational principles to be learned from these narratives, and some of these we have already studied. Our studies have pulled out select passages from the lives of the patriarchs. This small book is not at all comprehensive in searching for imbedded principles in those lives. Other biblical narratives could teach us other principles.

In the following discussions we will suggest a broader scope of partriarchal influence, but not study it in detail. We will review some of the principles highlighted in previous chapters. We will try to create a big-picture frame-of-reference and attempt to show these principles relevant to ourselves today.

The Patriarchs Extended
In this book, we have limited our look at the patriarchs of Israel to Abraham, Isaac, and Jacob. Those were the ones with whom God personally gave a covenant promise. They were the most foundational persons of the early called-out clan of the Hebrews. Abraham and Isaac both had other children, but those were not included in the covenant family. Jacob had twelve sons, and they were all included, by God's purpose. From each of these twelve sons came the twelve tribes of Israel, all of whom were considered part of the covenant nation. Thus, each of Jacob's sons were the patriarch of their successive tribe. In New Testament times Stephen recited this fact before the high priest.

Acts 7:8 (NIV2011)
⁸ Then he gave Abraham the covenant of circumcision. And Abraham became the father of Isaac and circumcised him eight days after his birth. Later Isaac became the father of

Jacob, and Jacob became the father of the twelve patriarchs.

We could pick out narratives from Genesis about each of the twelve sons, and extend our study of the patriarchs. Although there were twelve sons and twelve tribes in the messianic nation, the redemptive purpose, the messianic lineage, would only come through one of those tribes. Jacob prophesied this when he blessed his twelve sons just prior to his own death.

> *Genesis 49:1-2,8-12 (NKJV)*
> *¹ And Jacob called his sons and said, "Gather together, that I may tell you what shall befall you in the last days: ² "Gather together and hear, you sons of Jacob, And listen to Israel your father . . . ⁸ "Judah, you are he whom your brothers shall praise; Your hand shall be on the neck of your enemies; Your father's children shall bow down before you. ⁹ Judah is a lion's whelp; From the prey, my son, you have gone up. He bows down, he lies down as a lion; And as a lion, who shall rouse him? ¹⁰ The scepter shall not depart from Judah, Nor a lawgiver from between his feet, Until Shiloh comes; And to Him shall be the obedience of the people. ¹¹ Binding his donkey to the vine, And his donkey's colt to the choice vine, He washed his garments in wine, And his clothes in the blood of grapes. ¹² His eyes are darker than wine, And his teeth whiter than milk.*

In verses 3-7 and 13-25, omitted here, Jacob spoke to the other eleven sons and their tribes. He addressed all twelve according to their age, from oldest to youngest. This is often referred to as Jacob's "blessing" of his sons, but for most of them, the statements were not blessings, but curses. Only two of the twelve sons received a completely favorable prediction. Joseph was given the right of first-born, even though he was second from the youngest. Judah was designated as the princely tribe. These proclamations were not expressions of Jacob's feelings about his sons. They were prophetic destinies given from God. The key statement for us is that *the scepter shall not depart from Judah, Nor a lawgiver from between his feet, Until Shiloh comes; And to Him shall be the obedience of the people.* The scepter implies kingship, long before the chosen people even had a king. Shiloh is a reference to the Messiah, the ultimate king. The messianic lineage is prophesied to come through the tribe of Judah. Thus, the big picture is laid out, with the messianic path forward. In the New

Testament, looking back to the divine initiative, Paul recounts the legacy of being Jewish.

> Romans 9:4-5 (NIV2011)
> [4] *the people of Israel. Theirs is the adoption to sonship; theirs the divine glory, the covenants, the receiving of the law, the temple worship and the promises.* [5] *Theirs are the patriarchs, and from them is traced the human ancestry of the Messiah, who is God over all, forever praised! Amen.*

Israel Today

There is a great deal of disagreement today about the nation Israel. Obviously, there is hostility with her Islamic middle-eastern neighbors. But even within Christianity there is a divided perspective about how to regard the nation of Israel. One opinion believes that in New Testament times, the church has permanently replaced Israel as the chosen people, and that Israel is no longer significant in the remainder of God's dealings with mankind. This is called 'transfer' theology because it holds that all the unfulfilled promises of the Old Testament are seen as being transferred to the church in the New Testament. Today's so-called 'covenant theology' holds this view. The reason for this transfer, according to this view, is the rejection of their Messiah when they implemented his execution on the cross.

The competing opinion about Israel is that Israel has only been set aside temporarily, not permanently. This view holds that God is not finished with Israel yet, and that Israel will be restored to faith at the end of this age, becoming a significant player in end-of-the-age events. People calling themselves 'dispensationalists' hold this view.

This is a deep divide that cannot be addressed comprehensively in this book. I will just make a brief summary and statement so the reader can have a perspective for reading this book. The author holds to a dispensational viewpoint, based on an understanding of New Testament scripture. Covenant theology is a holdover of late middle-age thinking which considered Israel dead forever. It was born from unbelief, not from faith. Theologians lost hope of a restored Israel. They saw absolutely no possibility for a restored Israel after so long a time and generated this theology to cover for God's inability to fulfill His covenant promises to Israel. Most of reformed Christianity held this view prior to the last century.

But the Zionist movement began. It was an initiative to secure a Jewish homeland in the Palestine region and restore Israel as the rightful owner of that land. This movement was driven largely by Jewish influence in the United States and Great Britain. After World Wars I and II, that influence resulted in a redistribution of land in the Palestine region, defining a homeland for Israel. Many dispersed Jews returned once again to their homeland. In 1948, surrounded by hostile neighbors, Israel declared itself a political nation, then quickly defended its right through decisive, even miraculous, military victory.

As a result, a new hope for a literal restoration of Israel to faith in their Messiah, as prophesied in the Old Testament, now seems feasible. Out of that turn of events, the original Christian belief in a literal believing Israel at the time of Christ's return, has been revived in our day. For a more biblically comprehensive perspective on this view, the reader is referred to Romans, chapters 9, 10, and 11. The following exert summarizes things for us:

> *Romans 11:28-36 (NIV2011)*
> *[28] As far as the gospel is concerned, they [Jews] are enemies for your sake; but as far as election is concerned, they are loved on account of the patriarchs, [29] for God's gifts and his call are irrevocable. [30] Just as you who were at one time disobedient to God have now received mercy as a result of their disobedience, [31] so they too have now become disobedient in order that they too may now receive mercy as a result of God's mercy to you. [32] For God has bound everyone over to disobedience so that he may have mercy on them all. [33] Oh, the depth of the riches of the wisdom and knowledge of God! How unsearchable his judgments, and his paths beyond tracing out! [34] "Who has known the mind of the Lord? Or who has been his counselor?" [35] "Who has ever given to God, that God should repay them?" [36] For from him and through him and for him are all things. To him be the glory forever! Amen.*

We read in verse 29 that God's call to the patriarchs was *irrevocable*. Paul goes on to say that in the Old Testament, the Gentile nations were witnessed to by Israel. In the New Testament the Jews have gone to unbelief and are being witnessed to by believing Gentiles. God has bound all men over to unbelief in their own time, that He might have mercy on them all.

The message to us is this. The Jews are loved by God, not because they deserve it, but by His sovereign choice and for the fulfilling of His promises to the Patriarchs. We read in Chapter 1 that in God's covenant with Abraham, he promised blessing to any nations or peoples who would bless Israel and curses to any nations who opposed them. Since this promise is said to be irrevocable, it is still in force.

The United States has been Israel's greatest political ally since its fairly recent rebirth. However, that support has declined significantly over the last several decades and is seen as incidental by many in national leadership today. The craving for imported energy has coerced our leaders to lean more favorably toward the oil-exporting nations, those who are avowed enemies of Israel. If we don't continue to support Israel as God's unique nation, then we can expect more of the decline that is already occurring when God removes His hand of providential favor from us.

<u>Living in Hope</u>
We noted in Chapter 1 that Abraham was justified by faith when he believed the promises God gave to him. God counted his faith as righteousness, showing him mercy. God made a covenant with Abraham that promised a large posterity, one that would include the Messiah. Through this posterity and that Messiah, all people on earth would be blessed. Through this Messiah, salvation would come to all nations. Spiritually, all who believed in that promise, Jews and Gentiles, and in the Messiah would be counted as children of Abraham and would have salvation unto eternal life, as explained by Paul.

> *Romans 15:7-13 (NIV2011)*
> *[7] Accept one another, then, just as Christ accepted you, in order to bring praise to God. [8] For I tell you that Christ has become a servant of the Jews on behalf of God's truth, so that the promises made to the patriarchs might be confirmed [9] and, moreover, that the Gentiles might glorify God for his mercy. As it is written: "Therefore I will praise you among the Gentiles; I will sing the praises of your name." [10] Again, it says, "Rejoice, you Gentiles, with his people." [11] And again, "Praise the Lord, all you Gentiles; let all the peoples extol him." [12] And again, Isaiah says, "The Root of Jesse will spring up, one who will arise to rule over the nations; in him the Gentiles will hope." [13] May the God of hope fill*

you with all joy and peace as you trust in him, so that you may overflow with hope by the power of the Holy Spirit.

Isaiah 45:21-22 (NIV2011)
[21] Declare what is to be, present it— let them take counsel together. Who foretold this long ago, who declared it from the distant past? Was it not I, the LORD? And there is no God apart from me, a righteous God and a Savior; there is none but me. [22] "Turn to me and be saved, all you ends of the earth; for I am God, and there is no other.

Matthew 8:11 (NIV2011)
[11] I say to you that many will come from the east and the west, and will take their places at the feast with Abraham, Isaac and Jacob in the kingdom of heaven.

Phrases such as *all you ends of the earth* and *from the east and the west* speak of Gentiles--those who were not genetic offspring of covenant Israel, but were Abraham's spiritual offspring. This faith-principle carried powerfully into the New Testament. Jesus was surrounded by *the twelve*. On the night he was betrayed, he shared a New Covenant meal with his disciples, then prayed for them. As he prayed, he said this:

John 17:6-10,20-21 (ESV)
[6] "I have manifested your name to the people whom you gave me out of the world. Yours they were, and you gave them to me, and they have kept your word. [7] Now they know that everything that you have given me is from you. [8] For I have given them the words that you gave me, and they have received them and have come to know in truth that I came from you; and they have believed that you sent me. [9] I am praying for them. I am not praying for the world but for those whom you have given me, for they are yours. [10] All mine are yours, and yours are mine, and I am glorified in them . . . [20] "I do not ask for these only, but also for those who will believe in me through their word, [21] that they may all be one, just as you, Father, are in me, and I in you, that they also may be in us, so that the world may believe that you have sent me.

Those who believe the truth of God are counted as righteous, whether in Abraham's day or in our day. Abraham was the recipient of certain promises from God. Yet he died without receiving those promises. We learned in Chapter 1 that the patriarchs *only saw them and welcomed them from a distance, admitting that they were foreigners and strangers on earth.* They realized their true promised land was a heavenly country, and their real reward an eternal one. Likewise, we are called to live in this world, but not to be of this world. We too are just passing through this life on our way to our eternal reward. We are taught to live with a pilgrim mentality, setting our hearts on things above rather than things of this world.

Seeing the big picture, the wide-angle vision, the eternal perspective—that is the foundation of Christian hope in this world. Hope is one of the great driving forces of the faith. Biblical hope is not like that defined by today's normal usage of the word. Normal understanding would describe 'hope' as roughly equivalent to 'wish.' 'I hope I have enough gas in my tank to make it to the next gas station' is just a wish. In contrast, the hope of the Christian is always a product of faith. No hope is offered apart from faith. Hope is born in the revealed promises of God. But it means more than just believing in them. Hope means longing, yearning, setting your affections on them. My personal definition of biblical hope is 'faith plus longing.' Paul expresses it this way:

> *Romans 8:19-25 (NIV2011)*
> [19] *For the creation waits in eager expectation for the children of God to be revealed.* [20] *For the creation was subjected to frustration, not by its own choice, but by the will of the one who subjected it, in hope* [21] *that the creation itself will be liberated from its bondage to decay and brought into the freedom and glory of the children of God.* [22] *We know that the whole creation has been groaning as in the pains of childbirth right up to the present time.* [23] *Not only so, but we ourselves, who have the firstfruits of the Spirit, groan inwardly as we wait eagerly for our adoption to sonship, the redemption of our bodies.* [24] *For in this hope we were saved. But hope that is seen is no hope at all. Who hopes for what they already have?* [25] *But if we hope for what we do not yet have, we wait for it patiently.*

May the hope of the patriarchs be contagious to each of us. May they serve us as models of hopeful living, and their life struggles be examples to us. May we experience that inward groaning as we wait for the promised redemption to be consummated. That groaning is not a groaning of despair. It is a groaning of patient longing. That hope does not make us miserable in this life. No! Just the opposite. It gives us joy in this life, a joy that is not defined by our circumstances, but is anchored in our promised eternal reward.

> *Hebrews 6:19-20a (NIV2011)*
> [19] *We have this hope as an anchor for the soul, firm and secure. It enters the inner sanctuary behind the curtain,* [20] *where our forerunner, Jesus, has entered on our behalf. .*

> *Romans 15:4 (NIV2011)*
> [4] *For everything that was written in the past was written to teach us, so that through the endurance taught in the Scriptures and the encouragement they provide we might have hope.*

Hope looks to the eternal future. It anticipates the ultimate reward. It longs to be in the presence of our Creator. It brings a certain peace about death that is not available without it. Paul spoke of this unique peace in his letter to the Thessalonians.

> *1 Thessalonians 4:13 (NIV2011)*
> [13] *Brothers and sisters, we do not want you to be uninformed about those who sleep in death, so that you do not grieve like the rest of mankind, who have no hope.*

He is not saying that we do not grieve over death. He is saying we don't grieve in the same way that hopeless people do. There is a huge distinction between the outlooks of the hopeful and the hopeless. Paul could speak this way because he had fully contemplated the prospect of life and death, weighed each of them, and concluded this in another letter:

> *2 Corinthians 5:1-8 (ESV)*
> [1] *For we know that if the tent that is our earthly home is destroyed, we have a building from God, a house not made with hands, eternal in the heavens.* [2] *For in this tent we groan, longing to put on our heavenly dwelling,* [3] *if indeed by putting it on we may not be found naked.* [4] *For while we are still in this tent, we groan, being burdened—not that we would be unclothed, but that we would be further clothed, so that what is mortal may be swallowed up by life.* [5] *He who has prepared us for this very thing is God, who has*

given us the Spirit as a guarantee. ⁶ So we are always of good courage. We know that while we are at home in the body we are away from the Lord, ⁷ for we walk by faith, not by sight. ⁸ Yes, we are of good courage, and we would rather be away from the body and at home with the Lord.

Paul was not a philosopher. He was a realist who had been shown divine perspective. He had ordered his life around this belief, and had paid dearly as a result. Having been rejected, beaten, flogged, stoned, snake-bit, shipwrecked, imprisoned and mocked, he could lift his battle-scarred head and declare with confident and joyful proclamation that hope in Jesus was worth it all.

2 Corinthians 2:14a (ESV)
¹⁴ But thanks be to God, who in Christ always leads us in triumphal procession . . .

May this study of the patriarchs increase our dependency on eternity-focused hope.

In Summary
"Father Abraham had many sons; many sons had father Abraham. I am one of them and so are you, so let's just praise the Lord."

So goes the song generally sung by children at church camp or vacation bible school which teaches them that they too are part of God's covenant with Abraham as the father of all people having faith in the true God. This one verse of this children's song somehow seems to sum up the purpose of knowing and understanding the relationship between the Patriarchs and ourselves within God's spiritual world.

We first looked at God's covenant with Abraham and learned that it had a far greater meaning than land, flocks and posterity; it meant a lasting kinship with the Almighty. Next we observed the great faith and obedience Abraham displayed in the near sacrifice of his own son. We know that overcoming sin requires a special blood sacrifice but Isaac was not it. Instead we saw in that a foreshadow of Christ, *the lamb of God who takes away the sin of the world.* More importantly, we saw the transparent passion of God in redeeming a lost humanity. In that same episode, we also saw the obedience and loyalty of Jesus as portrayed by Isaac. Then we shared the vision of Jacob's dream where heavenly messengers were moving back and forth between heaven and earth to bridge the great divide between the two. Jesus was the ladder, the bridge, between them. Next we observed Jacob wrestling with God and began to understand the need for our own wrestling with God in prayer, so that we learn what it means to let him reign as Lord in our hearts. In all of these episodes, we saw the parallels between the Patriarchs and the Holy Father and His Son. The stories gave men and women veiled foreshadows of the Triune God. God had us in view when He gave these pictures in history. They connect us even more tightly with the Patriarchs and tie the Old and New Testaments together, while tying us more closely to God Himself.

Another Christian song declares, "Blessed be the tie that binds our hearts in Christian love." We are tied not only to present-day fellow worshippers, but to all who have believed and worshipped down through the ages. And we are tied to future generations of faithful believers. Through faith we are tied to the patriarchs. Of course, the crowning reality is that we are tied, along with all these others, to the God who created us for this very purpose. We are bound in intimate relationship to the Father, to Jesus the Son, and to the Holy Spirit. All of God and all of ourselves, the faithful, are bound together as one family for all eternity. Praise God forever!!

www.ingramcontent.com/pod-product-compliance
Lightning Source LLC
Chambersburg PA
CBHW071317040426
42444CB00009B/2035